MW00929558

Deeply Devoted

Grow intimacy with God
through daily devotions that
change your life and bring you joy

Deeply Devoted

**Grow intimacy with God
through daily devotions that
change your life and bring you joy**

Copyright © 2024, Deeply Devoted Resources

All quotations from the Bible are taken from
The Holy Bible: New International Version ® NIV®
Copyright © 1984 by International Bible Society

Acknowledgements

First of all, to my Shauna: Thank you for believing in me, supporting me, praying for me, loving me, and helping this dream to come true. You're the best!

I can't possibly thank everyone who has helped me grow in my faith over the years. That said, there are specific people in my life I want to honour—brothers and sisters who have modelled faith or intimacy with God clearly enough for me to catch it versus just reading about it.

I remember Charlie McCall and Bill Busshaus, Capernwray Bible School instructors whose passion for God's word both ignited and shaped my lifelong love for the scriptures way back in 1988/89.

Then there was Thom Koop, my feisty Youth Pastor, who showed me what an intimate walk with Jesus looks like in the life of a leader.

My world got rocked on a summer Mission Trip to Eastern Canada in 1991. Both Randy Friesen (the director of Youth Mission International at the time) and the late Steve Lightle (a messianic Jew) blew my mind with their supernatural intimacy with Jesus. Some of their globe-trotting God-exploits shifted world events in ways that made the cover of *Time Magazine*. They clearly marked a 'before-and-after' season for me.

I'm thankful for my dear friend and brother Norm Rempel. He walked with me through my darkest season and is now enjoying his Lord and Saviour in heaven, face to face.

I also need to honour my mom, who, despite the death of my dad in 2022, has leaned into Jesus during this season in beautiful ways.

An over-the-top thank-you to my new friend, Randy Carter, is also in order. He heard my heart for *Deeply Devoted* over coffee and was kind enough to say, "I think I'm supposed to help you." He was also crazy enough to put his money where his mouth went because Jesus told him to. I'm thankful to be part of the STM family to develop this *Deeply Devoted* as a ministry to the church.

Above all I honour my Lord Jesus. Your perfect life, death, and resurrection make my intimacy with your Father possible. Thank you with all I have, for all you are. I love you.

Inside this book

Introduction

If you've picked up this book, it's because you want to go deeper with God and you're looking for some help getting there.

Maybe you're brand new at this. The idea of intimacy with God feels a bit like the wild West—a potential gold rush, but the frontier feels so foreign that you don't know where to begin. Some kind of map might be nice, am I right?

Maybe you've got some history with God, but that's all you've got these days. Things have gone a little stale. You're doing what you know how to do, but you're ready to trade in your beige beliefs for faith in living colour.

Of course, you might be a passionate Jesus-lover. You already know God is the most beautiful, captivating, and liberating being in the universe and you can't get enough of him. You're hungry, ready, and I'm already moving too slow for you.

Many people seem content to live with head-knowledge *about* God. They believe in him and understand core biblical concepts, but don't know God through personal experience. They have a relationship *to* God, but don't enjoy a relationship *with* God.

Others go slightly deeper; for them, God isn't merely an idea or the abstract focal point of their faith. He has stepped out of the pages of scripture to become real in their actual experience. But while God is real to them, they rarely experience him in personal ways.

A third group of people enjoy a *personal* relationship with God. They understand God is pursuing them and enjoy his friendship in their daily experience. They read his word, are learning to hear God's voice, and draw great comfort and support from his love.

Still others enjoy an *intimate* relationship with God. It's not just that Jesus is a friend to them; they happily give themselves to be his friends in return. As a result, God confides in them. These people are not just believers. God is their first and true love. Their hearts burn for him, and their faces light up when they talk about him—and they talk about him a lot.

Last and rarest of all are the sacred souls for whom God has become *everything*. They want the Promise-giver more than his promises. They live, move, and breathe to give themselves to him. Their deepest longing is to behold and be held by him. That's the kind of person I want to be.

How would you describe your current relationship with God? Don't pretend, justify, or give yourself any slack. Own your current reality. As the Lord asked Adam after the Fall, "Where are you?" (Genesis 3:9) Wherever you're starting from, this book will take you deeper.

As I write this, my wife, Shauna, and I have been married for three decades. We enjoy a deep and satisfying friendship that has inspired many people over the years. People have often commented, "You're like a couple of newlyweds," or, "I wish I could have what you guys have."

Like many newlyweds, our honeymoon phase began with beauty and butterflies. Fast-forward six years into our married life, however, and the honeymoon had long gone. I was a Youth Pastor leading a growing youth group back then. Two rangy kiddos ran us ragged, with number three on the way. Life was crazy busy, we felt increasingly disconnected with each other, and our relationship was showing the strain.

I'll never forget one of our epic arguments. Shauna was driving, I can't remember where. We were fighting, I can't remember why. What I can remember is boiling over so desperately that I blurted out, "If you don't (insert immature demand), I'm going to jump out of this car!" Without so much as blinking an eye, she replied, "Go for it."

During this season—entire years were a blur back then, honestly—a beautiful couple in our church sat us down for a talk. "You guys need to go on regular dates and spend time alone together," they said. "We'll babysit your kids. What day works best for you?" The subtext stung a little: *your relationship is struggling, and you need to spend time together to fix it. We love you enough not to give you an option on this.*

Shauna and I got the hint. We took them up on their offer. Surprise, surprise—our relationship started deepening, one date at a time. Thirty years later, we still enjoy a weekly coffee date that's become a cornerstone of our love for each other. I wouldn't trade it for anything.

Is there more to our marriage than weekly coffee dates? Of course. The 'dates' actually aren't the point. It's what our dates make possible— connecting with each other—that's mined the lasting gold. Reserving this time for each other built a healthy rhythm of sharing, support, and love that we couldn't get any other way.

The same principle applies to our relationship with God. The best way to grow deeper intimacy with Jesus is to spend regular time alone with him. Like it or not, your "daily devotions," your "quiet time," or "God time"—I don't care what you call it—is the foundation of intimacy with Jesus.

Should our relationship with God go beyond daily devotions? Of course. Daily devotions are not the point. Walking with God is. It's just that without regular, one-on-one interaction with him, all the other things you long for in your relationship with God won't have anything to build on.

Saints throughout the scriptures understood this truth and grew their own deep roots by investing regular time alone with their Creator.

Moses enjoyed an intimacy with God that astounds me. What was his secret? He "used to take a tent and pitch it outside the camp some distance away, calling it the 'tent of meeting.'" Here, "the Lord would speak to Moses face to face, as one speaks to a friend" (Exodus 33:7, 11). Moses set aside regular time and space for God. He then reaped the jaw-dropping benefits of his daily investment.

Few of us will ever live as intimately with God as King David did. Listen to the warrior-poet's regular experience: "In the morning, Lord, you hear my voice; in the morning I lay my requests before you and wait expectantly" (Psalm 5:3). He also said, "One thing I ask from the Lord, this only do I seek: that I may dwell in the house of the Lord all the days of my life, to gaze on the beauty of the Lord and to seek him in his temple" (Psalm 27:4). Even amidst the relentless pressure of his kingly duties, David found time for God every day.

The Old Testament prophet Daniel is another notable example. He's famous for receiving mind-boggling visions from God, experiencing supernatural provision, and enjoying a sleepover in a den of lions. Daniel's mind captured deep downloads of divine wisdom that put government officials to shame. How was this possible? "Three times a day he got down on his knees and prayed, giving thanks to his God..." (Daniel 6:10).

Christ himself invested regular time connecting with his Father in heaven. This is significant, because Jesus enjoyed unbroken fellowship with God at every moment. He 'practiced God's presence' perfectly throughout the day, but still "often withdrew to lonely places and prayed" (Luke 5:16). Christ's ministry flowed directly from his time with his Father. "I do nothing on my own but speak just what the Father has taught me," Jesus said. "I am telling you what I have seen in the Father's presence" (John 8:28,38).

Christ assumed we'd be doing the same thing: "When you pray, go into your room, close the door, and pray to your Father, who is unseen" (Matthew 6:6). Some call this the secret place. We give our full attention to God, closing the door to outside distractions to focus on him alone.

Listen to Christ's words: "Just as the living Father sent me and I live because of the Father, so the one who feeds on me will live because of me" (John 6:53-57). This feeding is an ongoing action. When we're with Jesus, we partake of his essence, his power, his grace. There is no substitute for time alone with him. Grace is fully and freely given, but we partake of this grace by responding in faith.

I think you already know this stuff, but knowing isn't enough. Shauna and I knew things were going downhill in our relationship, but we didn't act on this knowledge. We needed the firmness of loving friends to press us towards fixing the problem. I'd like to be that person for you. So let me say it: It's time for you to go deeper with God by setting aside regular time to be with him alone, one on one.

But how does that work? Christians seem to struggle to keep a daily 'God-time' more than anything else! That's why I wrote *Deeply Devoted*. I want to help you develop a daily date with God that you enjoy, that deepens your intimacy with him, and changes your life.

Full disclosure: I can't babysit your kids to make scheduling your God-time easier (sorry). What I can do is show you how to connect with God on your daily dates with him. I'm confident that genuine intimacy with God will follow. Each chapter will close with a summary and reflection questions to apply what you learned.

In *Part One* of this book, I'll unpack three paradigm shifts you'll need to embrace to set your dates with God, keep them, and love them.

In *Part Two*, I'll walk you through a powerful biblical pathway designed by God to help you grow intimacy with him. We'll also talk about what to do 'after the amen,' including some traps to avoid.

In *Part Three*, I'll give you crash courses in powerful practices that will help you take your daily devotions to the next level: Bible Study, hearing God's voice, prayer journalling, and repentance. I'll also give you access to my online toolbox of resources and exercises you can use to take your relationship with God to the next level.

This book won't cover everything you need to know about growing intimacy with God. I'm certainly not claiming daily devotions are the only way intimacy develops. But it bears repeating: The best way to grow deeper intimacy with Jesus is to spend regular time alone with him. We simply have to figure that out.

Here's my promise to you: If you track with me through these pages and put them into practice, you will develop a daily date with God you'll love. You will grow a deeper intimacy with him. And it will change your life.

I feel a little like little Lucy from *The Lion, The Witch, and the Wardrobe* right now. Like her, I've stumbled onto something like a magical wardrobe that's opened up a whole new world. Now I'm trying to convince you (my brothers and sisters) that there really is a land called Narnia waiting for us. Boldest and best of all, I'm saying that Aslan is waiting just through the door, eager for us to answer his call.

Pray with me. Try something like this:

> "Father in heaven, I want to go deeper with you—but honestly, part of me resists it. Another part of me shrinks back from moving closer to you because I don't know how. I desperately want this book to help me, so I can have more of you. Please, Holy Spirit, come guide me into all truth. Lord Jesus, take me where you want me to go, change what you want to change in me as my Lord and Saviour. Amen."

1

What's Our Problem?

A while back I posted a question to my Facebook friends. I thought it might help me write this book, and I wasn't disappointed:

"What is your greatest struggle when it comes to doing your daily devotions?"

You'd probably resonate with their responses, but take a moment to reflect on how you would answer the question. *What's your greatest struggle with daily devotions?*

Got it?

I love how one guy responded:

"Doing them."

The conversation that unfolded over the next few days in the comments was raw and real. As the dialog continued, I collected some valuable insights into the struggles most Christians experience in their quiet times. Their input helped me distill five common 'disconnect points' that make it hard for Christians to keep up a daily devotional routine.

You can probably relate to at least a few of them.

1. We struggle to maintain healthy motivation

Apathy is addictive. It's far too easy to drift numbly through days, weeks, and even months without giving God much focused one-on-one time. We're far better at making it look like we care than actually caring. And while spending time with Jesus would help us cope with life more effectively, we're used to handling things mostly on our own. We haven't totally tanked yet, so we keep on keeping on. We pitch ourselves the lie that we'll become more devoted to Jesus in a tomorrow that never comes.

Many Christians live with a sense that they're letting God down because they don't 'do' daily devotions. Failing in our daily time with God gradually saddles us with an underlying guilt. Guilt that isn't dealt with often leads to shame: *it's not just that I'm failing God; I'm a failure to God.* Guilt and shame are toxic motivations for spending time with Jesus. They can only create a legalistic (rule-based) approach that strangles genuine passion.

2. We struggle to find, make, and keep the time

Your schedule is already full, and it already tires you out. Am I right? We're always just a little too busy to add one more thing to our schedules. We feel overworked. We're chronically tired. Countless issues and responsibilities nag for our attention and wait impatiently for our follow-through. There are always other things to do, and those other things often feel more important (or fun!) at the moment than sitting down to read our Bibles and pray.

I'm lookin' at you, Instagram.

Life has a way of filling up whatever schedule we attempt to keep. Spending time with God requires reclaiming time from other things. If we somehow find a few minutes (in theory) for daily devotions, it's hard to make it work long term. If we're getting up early to pray, morning fights back with a vengeance. Our kiddos revolt to reclaim our highest priority. Our to-do list gnaws away at our gut and lies to us: *You can spend time with God later.* But we don't, do we?

Making time for God is a battle because it's important. You may want to read that again.

3. We can't seem to stay focused

It's no secret that our social feeds and online media dole out dopamine hits and suck us into their bottomless vortex. But did you know they're re-wiring our brains on a neurological level? Every technology gives us something while taking something away. The printed page gave us the ability to capture ideas outside of our brains. The tradeoff? Over time, we stopped using our brains to store everything we needed to know. We became dependent on the printed page to remember things for us. In the same way, thousands of hours online have trained our brains to focus on shiny, sexy, and exciting things in seven-second bursts.

If by some divine miracle we're able to sit down with a candle lit, our coffee steaming, and our Bible open, something will almost always interrupt our focus. Our phone will bing, ring, or sing. Our kids will need help to find their rogue sock. We'll remember that we forgot to add that appointment to our calendar.

I've disabled notifications for most of my apps, but they still bug me. Awhile back I dug into my daily summary and found that I'd received twenty-seven text notifications, sixteen calendar notifications, two phone calls, and nine Messenger notifications for the past day. According to Zippia.com, "The average American checks their phone 96 times per day, or once every ten to twelve minutes," also noting that "we actually touch our phones up to 2,617 times per day and unlock our phones 150 times on average."

If that weren't bad enough, while we check our phone, we also check our Instagram feed—really quickly, just a few swipes. Or X, TikTok,

YouTube, and Facebook—until we've flushed our entire God-time into our social toilet. Or maybe you have trouble focusing on one thing for more than a few minutes at a time. For many people, deep, biblical meditation feels like an elite activity for people who are way more spiritual than they are.

4. We feel stifled by approaches to daily devotions that don't fit how we're wired

Maybe reading—including the Bible—feels like pulling teeth to you. Perhaps expressing your feelings makes you uncomfortable. Maybe you hate writing, so prayer journalling sounds like water torture. Some people hate singing, or don't connect with music. If you're an extrovert, getting alone with God might feel lonely. For some, pre-written devotional books become soul-stifling boxes. For others, not working through a guided devotional feels like facing a choose-your-own-adventure fiasco. Some people want to figure things out on their own; others want to be told what to do and how to do it.

When the particular mode of daily devotions we're attempting presses us into a mold that seems at odds with who we are, we may find it difficult to engage and enjoy our time with God.

5. We get little out of our devotions and end up quitting—or just going through the motions

The cumulative result of these four disconnects is a devotional time that falls (and feels) flat. I've lost count of how many times I've heard people confess Bible study feels empty or dull to them. More people than you know feel like they get precious little out of their time with God.

Progress helps us persevere. It's nearly impossible to keep up a discipline that doesn't produce tangible benefits over time. Those that keep up a daily devotion routine may end up going through the motions.

Some people persevere because dropping their quiet times would stir up those feelings of guilt and shame again.

Can you can relate to any of these struggles? If you're not sure what's gone wrong or how to fix it, you've got company. You are one of many millions of Christians trapped in an experience of devotional disconnect.

You can probably see by now that for your experience to change with God, you'll need to address these 'disconnect points.' The thing is, daily devotions are *weird*. Think about it:

• We're supposed to *get alone* to spend time with Someone

• We're called to grow intimacy with a God we can't hear, see, or touch

• There are specific motions we're supposed to go through, but we're not supposed to go through the motions

• We need to do this every day, without letting our routine become a rut

This may sound discouraging, but I have good news! A powerful truth also emerged from my Facebook conversations: *some people don't struggle with daily devotions.* Like, there are actually believers out there who enjoy their daily time with Jesus. They love it so deeply, they wouldn't miss it for the world.

I am one of those people.

The daily-devotion-lover's experience with Jesus isn't the fruit of a special flavour of favour from God not accessible to mere mortals. Our devotional delight is not the result of trying harder than other people. We don't taste more fruit from our quiet times because we're more disciplined, more spiritual, or more articulate than other Christians. So what's the difference?

Let me share a story to illustrate.

One day I was out doing errands and noticed my passenger-side windshield wiper was leaving streaks on the windshield. What did I do? Absolutely nothing! For a while, at least.

After months of pointless muttering while straining to see through a badly streaked windshield, I was finally ready to solve the problem. (By the way, whenever we refuse to solve a problem, we've become the problem).

Anyway, I dropped in to my local Canadian Tire and found the wiper aisle A handy touchscreen interface guided me through selecting the right wipers for my make, model, and year of car. I was finally fixing my problem by becoming the solution. I truly was *the man.*

When I arrived home, I unboxed the crisp new blades and got to work. I started with the main wiper, the big one on the driver's side. It required clipping a small adapter onto the existing wiper arm, after which the new blade clicked into place. That 'click' was so satisfying, and the fresh blade worked perfectly! What a relief.

Next up: repeating the same process with the real culprit, my passenger-side wiper. I took out the adapter clips provided and cycled through them, trying to find the one that fit. None of them worked. No matter how hard I tried pressing, squeezing, or popping, there was no 'click.' I couldn't make the wiper connect to the arm. Worst of all, I'd already lost the receipt, so I couldn't return the blade for a new one.

It doesn't fit my car, I mused. But at least I was now enjoying a beautiful wiper on the driver's side. That's what I told myself, so I could sleep at night.

A month-and-a-half later, the passenger portion of the windshield was even more streaked and dirty. The misfit wiper blade package was still stowed behind the passenger seat in my car, mocking me, daring me to do something about it.

Finally admitting defeat, I returned to the store, frustrated that I had to buy a new wiper blade to replace the wrong one. I stepped back up to the touchscreen and slogged through the same selection process. To my surprise, I received instructions to buy exactly the same wiper blade I'd bought the first time!

Sighing to myself, I returned to my car. I would marshal one last attempt to attach the renegade blade in my back seat. Surely I was missing something. But what? I cycled through the adapters again, carefully trying various approaches to making them fit. Once again, no go. The wiper didn't work. No satisfying click. Argh.

Unless...

Unless the passenger side didn't require an adapter. I tried again, sans adapter, and the stupid thing clicked instantly into place. Hurrying to the driver's seat, I hit the windshield with a fresh stream of washer fluid and watched both wipers work their glorious magic. Sparkling success!

I laughed at myself as I realized there was nothing wrong with the new blade. There never had been. I hadn't muttered through months of dirty windshields because the wiper blade didn't fit, but *because of the way I was seeing the problem.* The solution had been right in front of me all along, eluding the clutches of my little brain because of my approach to installing it.

Let's bring this home. Christians whose daily devotions 'click' with such satisfaction *approach their God-time differently than other people do.* Their approach opens up regular and rewarding experiences with God, while most people's approach dooms them to frustration and failure.

You may have tried all this devotional stuff before. Maybe for you, nothing clicks, fits, or cleans your proverbial windshield. You might have even concluded that the deeper 'God-stuff' is not for you and resigned yourself to live with a muddled view. But if you changed how you see daily devotions—if you adjusted how you approach them to match how God has designed them to work—they'd 'click' for you too. Devotions would become deeply meaningful to you, maybe even *instantly.*

I get it, you're skeptical. Let me tell you a bit more about myself to build some credibility here.

The first thing you need to know about me is that I'm kind of a bonehead. I'm artsy, emotional, stubborn, independent, and easily distracted. I struggle to follow through on things, get easily frustrated, and I hate doing the same activities repeatedly.

That said, Jesus captured my heart at eighteen. Ever since, I've made spending time with him a supremely important investment in my life. My "God-time" routine began in 1988 on sun-baked afternoons at Bible School in Comfort, Texas. While most of my friends headed down to the pool to cool off and catch some rays after lunch, I slipped away to bask in the presence of God. Since that season, most of my most treasured moments with him have unfolded during my quiet times.

I experience the love and grace of God in tangible ways when I spend time with him. I routinely hear the Lord's voice and gain his perspective on my life. His written word re-shapes my thinking, alters my decisions, and multiplies the effect my life has on others. I'm slowly becoming more like Jesus, and I'm progressively learning to live from my new self in Christ. I let go of my burdens and find freedom from fear, sin, and demonic attacks. Drawing from this freedom, I pray with faith, am led by the Spirit, and surrender myself to God's plan for me. When I'm done, I routinely find myself refreshed, focused, and full of faith and peace. Best of all, I'm getting to know God better.

My deepening intimacy with Jesus has nothing to do with my strengths. It grows directly from *my approach to interacting with him.* The same has been true for countless Jesus-loving people throughout the ages. This book will empower you with a powerful approach to daily devotions. Along the way, it will adjust your personal filters, mindset, expectations, and your goals. As that shift happens, you'll move from devotional disconnect to the delight of true intimacy. He really is the most magnificent and captivating being in the universe!

Don't worry; you won't need a seminary degree to make this work. You don't even have to be particularly intelligent, spiritual, or self-disciplined (I'm not!). What you will need is a commitment to be fully and unapologetically *yourself*.

I'm also going to ask you to approach this book as a student. Much of what you believe about daily devotions has been killing your quiet times and dooming them to failure. I can hardly wait to dismantle this stuff so I can help you connect with God like you've always longed for.

No more muddy windshield for you! Those wiper blades are going to click, and they're going to work like a charm. Your intimacy with God will start growing, and before you know it, you'll wonder how you survived without it.

For now, please pause to pray. Tell God you want this. Tell him you need his help. Invite him to do what he needs to do within you to make this work. I'll wait. :)

Part One:
Paradigm Shifts

2

Shift One: Initiating vs. Responding

The biggest difference between people who enjoy a rich daily devotional experience and those who don't is how they approach intimacy in the first place.

People who don't enjoy their time alone with God tend to see it as something they *ought* to do or *have to* do because that's what's required. People who relish their time alone with God view it as something they *want* and *need to* do because they love him and depend on what he provides.

Ought-to people often approach daily devotions as something they must initiate in order to convince God to respond to them. When they spend time with God, they're trying to get his attention. Daily devotions are their way of convincing God to bless them, speak to them, guide them, or connect with them. Deep down, *ought-to people* believe prayer and Bible study entitle them to get more from Jesus. I've been there, and it wasn't fun.

In contrast, *want-to people* tend to view their daily devotions as an ongoing, natural *response* to an attentive and loving God already pursuing them. They know God is already present, active, and waiting for them to tune in. He isn't the missing piece; they are.

That's how Moses thought.

Millenia ago, God liberated the Hebrew people from centuries of bondage to cruel Egyptian overlords. During that season of liberation, God's presence was tangible, even visible, among them. He shepherded them through the Wadi wasteland with pillars of fire and smoke. The Lord gifted them with ten commandments supernaturally inscribed on tablets of stone. He even satisfied their hunger pangs with manna and miracles.

The Hebrews understood then what most of us miss today—God being 'with' us is not the same as God being everywhere. The thought of losing this daily, manifest experience terrified them (Exodus 33:4,15). But even amid God's tangible presence, Moses went deeper with him than anyone else:

> "Moses used to take a tent and pitch it outside the camp some distance away, calling it the "tent of meeting." Anyone inquiring of the Lord would go to the tent of meeting outside the camp. And whenever Moses went out to the tent, all the people rose and stood at the entrances to their tents, watching Moses until he entered the tent. As Moses went into the tent, the pillar of cloud would come down and stay at the entrance, while the Lord spoke with Moses. Whenever the people saw the pillar of cloud standing at the entrance to the tent, they all stood and worshiped, each at the entrance to their tent. The Lord would speak to Moses face to face, as one speaks to a friend" (Exodus 33:7-11)

This inspires me so much! Moses did something none of his fellow Hebrews dared to do. He responded to God's presence among them by reciprocating by faith. Moses went deeper with God because he wanted more of him and put that desire into action. He responded to God's initiative by setting up a time, a place, and a space to meet with his Creator.

Anyone could make use of this tent. Interestingly enough, while others could, it appears as though only Moses did—at least regularly. Most people only visited the tent when they needed something. They sought an audience with God to obtain his blessing or breakthrough in their lives. Like many of us, they prayed when they were in trouble.

Moses didn't approach God that way. God's presence in the camp enamoured him. It stirred up a desire for more of his glory. Moses set up his tent as his faith response to what God was already doing. He consistently leaned in to interact with his King. As a result, he experienced something no one else did: a face-to-face friendship with the Lord of the cosmos.

No, Moses didn't earn these encounters by being a better Hebrew than anyone else. God explains later in this story,

> "I will cause all my goodness to pass in front of you, and I will proclaim my name, the Lord, in your presence. I will have mercy on whom I will have mercy, and I will have compassion on whom I will have compassion" (Exodus 33:19).

God doesn't respond to our works; he initiates with grace and mercy and awaits our response.

That said, Moses consistently responded to God's mercy by showing up before him. He asked for a greater revelation of both God's ways and his glory because he knew it would deepen their friendship (Exodus 33:13,18). Moses put himself in a position where he was ready to receive more of God if God decided to move. God replied, "I will do the very thing you have asked, *because I am pleased with you and I know you by name*" (Exodus 33:17).

Don't miss this: Most people settled for a corporate "God is among us." Moses went deeper by responding by faith. As a result, he experienced an intimate "face to face."

It gets better: The Hebrew words for 'face' and 'presence' are forms of the same word. The literal translation of Exodus 33:19, "I will proclaim my name... *in your presence*" is, "*in your face.*" So when God and Moses met "face to face," they met *presence to presence.* God had taken the initiative by becoming present to the people; *Moses responded by making himself fully present to God.*

It was never about the tent. It was about Moses' consistent and heartfelt faith response to God's initiative. God and Moses enjoyed deeper intimacy because they became mutually present to each other.

The scriptures clearly teach that we receive God's grace by faith (Ephesians 2:8,9). That's why Jesus said things like, "Let it be done to you according to your faith" (Matt. 9:29). On several occasions, he even stated, "Your faith has healed you" (Matthew 9:22, Mark 5:34, 10:52). It is God who heals by his grace—but his healing often arrives through faith. "By grace... through faith" may just be the most important principle of God's kingdom (Ephesians 2:8).

Many Christians assume the "God-stuff" is going to just fall in their laps, with no fresh faith required. They think if an experience is truly from God, it will be so loud and convincing that it won't take any faith to receive. Others seem to think that as they become more spiritual, they will need less faith because they will have such clear vision. This isn't a biblical idea. Faith can't achieve grace, but it is necessary to receive it.

According to my Keyword Study Bible, the first sense of the word *receive* means "to take with the hand, lay hold of, in order to use something." The second sense of the word means "to take what is one's own, to take to one's self, to make one's own, to claim." As you can see, receiving is an action. Jesus said, "Whatever you ask for in prayer, believe that you have received it"—have taken hold of it—"and it will be yours" (Mark 11:24).

God illustrates the active nature of receiving through the story of Israel crossing the Jordan River to claim their promised land. His conquering grace was available for the first generation who arrived at the muddy banks of the Jordan River. The Lord had promised the people, "I will give into your hands the people who live in the land, and you will drive them out before you" (Exodus 23:31). Unfortunately, they didn't press in to claim their promise. All but two of them—Joshua and Caleb—died off in the wilderness.

Forty years later, a new generation of Hebrews faced the same occupied territory. This time, when Joshua declared, "The Lord has surely given the whole land into our hands," the people believed him (Joshua 2:24). Even though the territory was still occupied, God's grace enabled them to envision a different reality: the land was already theirs, ready for the taking. To receive it, they simply needed to act—to step out in faith to take hold of what God had already provided.

The Apostle James wrote, "Faith by itself, if it is not accompanied by action, is dead... faith without deeds is useless" (James 2:17,20). The conquest of Jericho was an act of receiving what God was achieving. Receiving is an act of faith that moves God's blessings from his heart into my hands.

How does this understanding of receiving shape your intimacy with God? What you have faith to receive frames the depth of your relationship with God. You must take hold of what God has given through active obedience.

There is a vast difference between praying, "God, are you there?" and declaring, "God, I praise you for flowing in and through me right now. I know you are speaking and want to have a conversation with me. So let's start. What would you like me to know?"

The Holy Spirit is speaking to you, but if you don't believe it, you're going to have a hard time hearing him.

Jesus loves you, but if you don't believe it, you probably won't feel his love.

The Father is generous and kind, but if you think of him as a miserly old man, you won't find joy in serving him.

God's favour is already upon you in Christ. If you think you have to earn it, you'll spend your whole life trying to achieve what's already yours.

God is with you, but if you don't believe it, you probably won't set up a time, place, and space to meet with him.

Our God always goes first. Christ became human—lived and suffered and died—to bring you home to meet his Father. He's forgiven you, validated you, restored you, and honoured you with a seat in the heavenly places with him. He made you one with himself so he could tabernacle with you, moving in to make himself at home in the very core of your being. His Spirit flows within you to complete you. He flows out of you like streams of living water to bless the world. You are a branch on the Vine, a child fully embraced by his heart, the object of his affection and attention, the one he'd rather die for than live without. He's speaking to you, he's not holding anything back, he's working for your good...

...And, as A. W. Tozer remarked, "He waits to be wanted. Too bad that with many of us he waits so long, so very long, in vain." The Apostle James instructs us to "Come near to God and he will come near to you" (James 4:8). The message is clear: God went first, but what happens next depends on how we respond to him. This is the difference between God being a friend to you, and you becoming a friend to God.

Boom. More on that in the next chapter.

What Jesus has given you is not your finish line. It's your starting block. He showers you with his love, favour, authority, and unspeakable access, *so that*... *So that* you can draw near to him. *So that* you can enjoy his freedom. *So that* you can have conversations with him. *So that* you can learn to live in the delight of the Father, expand his kingdom, and make a real difference in eternity. It's all about intimacy.

This gets intensely practical. When you sit down to spend time with Jesus, you're not initiating, you're responding. Don't waste a single second trying to connect with God, earn his favour, or sound spiritual. Before you pray a single word, you are an accepted, validated, loved, seated, filled, blessed, and destined son or daughter of the Most High God with full (pre-glory) access to the courts of heaven. Everything else should flow from that powerful posture.

You don't *have to* spend time with God every day. You *get to* spend time with him every day. You don't need to get God's attention; he's trying to capture yours. He's already present. He's waiting for you to become present to him. You just... maybe don't know how.

Trust me, it's coming. But first, we need to set some relationship goals.

Key points from this chapter:

• People who struggle with daily devotions tend to see them as something they *have* to do in order to please God.

• People who love their daily devotions tend to see them as something they *get* to do as a faith response to a God who's already taken the initiative and is eagerly awaiting their response.

• **Q:** *Without trying to make yourself sound more spiritual, which kind of person describes you better—struggling with daily devotions, or loving them?*

• God is seeking an intimate relationship with us. To experience intimacy with him, we need to set aside a time, space, and place to meet with him regularly, like Moses did.

• **Q:** *Do you set aside a time, space, and place for God? Why or why not?*

• Our expectations—what we have faith to receive—frame the depth of our intimacy with God.

• **Q:** *What do you usually expect from your time alone with God, both positive and negative? Is there anything you sense needs to change about that after reading this chapter?*

• God waits to be wanted.

• **Q:** *How does that quote stir you? What will you do about it?*

3

Shift Two: Relationship Goals

In my early twenties, I often spent two or three hours per day in my quiet times. My wife can attest to how many Sunday mornings she'd be dressed for success, all coffee-d up, poised to walk out the door for church—only to find me lounging around un-showered, wrapped up in my bathrobe, still doing my 'devos.' I can still see her standing in the doorway of my office, eyes glazed over with confusion, sputtering.

"It's... almost time to leave. Like, now. I'm ready."

"Almost done," I'd say, grinning sheepishly.

That sounds pretty spiritual, right? God before showering, even. When I look back on those days, I'm so thankful they're behind me. I see now that my killer zeal resulted in self-effort and self-righteousness. I didn't know what a quiet time *was*, which meant I didn't grasp *the purpose of what I was doing*. As a result, I wasted far too much time and energy doing things God wasn't asking me to do.

In the end, my devotions sucked the life out of me instead of infusing me with Jesus. I kid you not, my daily devotions burned me out! It took years of re-framing to find myself at home in God's presence again. If you've ever dreaded doing your devotions, you know some of what I mean.

I've learned the hard way that it's impossible to develop a rich devotional life and intimacy with Jesus if you're starting with the wrong assumptions. So let me ask you some foundational questions:

- What *are* daily devotions?
- What is the *purpose* of daily devotions?
- What is supposed to be *happening* to you as a result?

Most people have never asked those questions. We don't know where we're going or how to get there, so we focus on what we know—hoping it adds up to something: Bible study, prayer, confession, worship. Or we stack these activities into slick acronyms, like A.C.T.S.—Adoration, Confession, Thanksgiving, and Supplication. Truthfully, we don't really know how to how to do these things either, which leads us to depend on devotional books written by others who seem to have it all figured out.

When people purchase a gym membership, they do lots of different exercises (none of which I enjoy, I should confess):

- Rowing
- Bicep curls
- Bench press
- Running on a treadmill
- Muttering into mirrors

You could add all kinds of exercises to this list. But the *goal* of a gym membership isn't rowing or arm curls. Doing these exercises in succession creates a workout, but workouts aren't the goal either. The goal, for me at least, is a healthy body that looks reasonably not-awful. When we stick with the program, we develop muscle tone, build our core strength, improve our cardio, get more ripped, or even just stay physically fit instead of turning into marshmallow pies.

In the same way, spiritual exercises like Bible reading, prayer, and worship are vitally important. We call this collection of exercises a *quiet time,* or *daily devotions.* But daily devotions aren't the goal. As we create a routine of meeting with God, it's meant to become more than the sum of the parts. It's supposed to translate into cumulative benefits for our spiritual health and growth. But self-improvement isn't the goal either—or rather, it shouldn't be.

Until you understand what a daily devotion time *is,* what *purpose* it fulfills in your life, and what's supposed to be *happening* to you as a result, you will never really gain traction in your daily devotions. So here's my working definition of a daily quiet time or daily devotions:

Daily devotions are a regular block of time set apart for personal interaction with God.

Every believer in Jesus has a relationship with Jesus. A relationship means two people are interacting: talking, listening, and responding to each other. What should occur during every quiet time is *personal, real-time interaction with God.* There should always be some kind of back-and-forth experience playing out between the two of you.

If you don't focus on interacting with God, you'll settle for much less. It's possible to read the Bible without interacting with God (the teachers of the law in Jesus' day did that). You can pray the most impressive-sounding prayers without interacting with God (the Pharisees pulled that off somehow). If you're not interacting with Jesus, you're just doing the equivalent of a spiritual workout, thinking *about* God without relating to him as a real, live *Person.*

Which brings us to the next question: What's the *purpose* of interacting with God through our daily devotions? In my twenties, I would start each daily devotion time with the assumption that I was not connected with God until I reached out to him. In my mind, the purpose of my daily devotion routine was to re-connect with God each morning. Maybe you can relate.

This faulty assumption led to another issue: If connecting with him was the purpose of my quiet time, then the only way to know whether my daily devotions were successful was *sensing* a connection with him. Feeling his presence become proof-positive that I had made that all-important connection. The real reason I spent so much time with God each day was that it often took a long time to feel like I'd connected with Jesus. Sometimes I didn't feel him at all, so I had to give up—pressing on with my day, feeling dejected and disconnected.

I meant well, but I did not offer my passion and devotion *in view of God's mercy.* It took me years to realize God has already connected me with him in Christ. My job is not to *create* that connection, but to *explore* it. This is the message of John 15, one of my favourite passages, where Jesus explains he is the Vine and we're the branches. We can summarize the subtext of that entire analogy like this: "You are connected to me. Live like it."

Today, when I sit down with Jesus, I begin *in view of God's mercy.* I remind myself of the spiritual connection with the Father Jesus sealed for me by shedding his blood. I smile, knowing this union doesn't depend on me to maintain. What used to be the finish line is now my starting block. As a result, my God-time is deeper, more meaningful, and more life-changing than ever. To get what Jesus gives, we have to start where Jesus finished—his salvation work that opened up full access to his Father.

If a daily quiet time is about interacting with God—an unnervingly real, glorious, powerful and vibrant Person—then your quiet time is never just about you. There are two distinct people engaged in every meeting, each bringing unique desires and goals to the table. One of these people—God—is infinitely more powerful, holy, worthy and wise than the other. I say this because most people come to God with their own agenda. We rarely consider what he might desire for our time together.

Thankfully, we find our highest relationship goals in Romans 12:1,2.

> "I urge you, brothers and sisters, in view of God's mercy, to offer your bodies as a living sacrifice, holy and pleasing to God—this is your true and proper worship. Do not conform to the pattern of this world, but be transformed by the renewing of your mind. Then you will be able to test and approve what God's will is—his good, pleasing and perfect will."

The Father's goal is to transform you into his image so he can have you for himself. He is tirelessly working to renew your mind, will, and emotions so that you become more and more like Jesus in every area of life. This is his will for you, and he's promised to finish what he started (Philippians 1:6). God's will is not just something to 'do.' It's someone to become, and that becoming is your destiny in Christ (Romans 8:29).

Your goal for your time alone with God should not be to learn something, feel something, read the Bible, or to pray. Your goal should be to give yourself more fully to God so he can accomplish his will in you. God wants all of you. Your job is to put yourself more completely on his altar as a living sacrifice of worship. As you do this, your relationship deepens.

As you place yourself in God's hands, the scripture says, he will gradually accomplish his will—his good, pleasing, and perfect destiny for you. Please pause on this truth for a beat: A 'successful' devotional time isn't one where I get something out of God; it's where God gets something out of me. Everything—and I mean everything—is about deepening our intimacy with God by giving ourselves more fully to him.

God is at work in every moment of your day, but your devotional time is *quality time* set apart especially for him. The Father will infuse those sacred moments with a grace that exerts a disproportionately powerful effect on the rest of your life. If you spend fifteen minutes interacting with God and you emerge more fully his, loving and trusting him even just a little more, that's a home run. Moses carried God's presence so powerfully throughout his life because he gave himself to God's presence whenever he could, for as long as he could. That should be our goal, too.

Mary (Martha's sister) is one of my New Testament heroes. Her posture towards Jesus uniquely embodies the beauty and simplicity of what giving ourselves to God is all about. Did you know that every time she appears in a Gospel story, we find her at Christ's feet?

In Luke 10:39, she "sat at the Lord's feet listening to what he said." When Martha complained about her sister's lack of help in the kitchen, Jesus replied, "Mary has chosen what is better, and it will not be taken away from her" (Luke 10:42). May we choose what is better, too.

In John 11:32, "she (Mary) fell at his feet," overcome with grief at the death of her brother, Lazarus. "Lord, if you had been here, my brother would not have died," she exclaimed (John 11:32). "When Jesus saw her weeping... he was deeply moved in spirit and troubled" (John 11:33). Her raw grief, poured out at his feet, struck such a chord within him that "Jesus wept" (John 11:34). I want to give Jesus my deepest aching and angst as well.

And finally, in John 12:3, when Christ's time on earth was drawing to a close, Mary "took about a pint of pure nard, an expensive perfume; she poured it on Jesus' feet and wiped his feet with her hair." When his disciples scoffed at this lavish and 'wasteful' expression of affection and devotion, he rebuked them. "Leave her alone," Jesus replied. "It was intended that she should save this perfume for the day of my burial"

(John 12:7). I want to be the person who worships Jesus with that kind of reckless abandon.

What Mary gave Jesus in these moments was deeply precious to him. Throughout these stories, Mary gave Jesus her full attention (her trust) and her deepest affection (her love). This is profound. The two haunting questions God poses repeatedly throughout the scriptures, either explicitly or implied, are, "Do you trust me?" and "Do you love me?" Mary's words and actions offered her Lord a resounding "Yes! I trust you and I love you."

When you give God your full attention and deepest affection, two equally important gifts for God become possible: dependence and obedience.

Your daily devotions help you renew your full dependence on Jesus. It's a space to press pause on the never-ending demands of your life to sink your roots deep into Christ and draw life from his love and truth (Ephesians 3:14-19). Here you can revel as a tender branch drawing life from his eternal Vine. Without him, you can do nothing and would wither spiritually (John 15:5,6).

Abiding in Christ throughout the day is impossible without laying the foundation of regular, face-to-face interaction with God in prayer. I need to pause and 'check in' throughout the day to renew my focus, affection, and dependence on Jesus.

Predictably, our pride resists this sanctifying work. Our quiet time is where we put that pride to death. We surrender our will to the Father and trust him with our life, like Jesus did in the garden of Gethsemane (Matthew 26:39, Hebrews 5:8). We refuse to lean on our own understanding, submitting our broken thinking to his word for "teaching, for reproof, for correction, and for training in righteousness" (II Timothy 3:16).

Jesus is the Truth; we are not. Our surrender to God's word progressively makes us "complete, equipped for every good work" (II

Timothy 3:17). As we receive guidance and conviction from him, we simply do what he's telling us to do. We obey him, no matter how loudly our flesh screams in defiance, and we keep obeying him. Jesus said discipleship is about learning "to obey everything I have commanded you" (Matthew 28:18-20). We are becoming obeyers—walking manifestations of the good, pleasing, and perfect will of God (Romans 12:1,2).

Attention. Affection. Dependence. Obedience.

These are 'the big four,' the essential building blocks for a life of faith. If God has your attention, affection, dependence, and obedience, he has *you*. His Spirit is free to work on you, in you, and through you. When you put yourself fully at his disposal, the kingdom comes and God's will is done. Daily devotions are God's sacred workshop—a time, space, and place where you can put yourself on the altar so he can have, hold, and change you.

The peace and joy I feel when God gets his way with me is beautiful. The Apostle Peter puts it so well. He writes, "Though you have not seen him, you love him; and even though you do not see him now, you believe in him and are filled with an inexpressible and glorious joy, for you are receiving the end result of your faith, the salvation of your souls." (I Peter 1:8,9). When I read these words, I want to shout, "Yes! This!"

Giving ourselves more fully to God is infinitely worth it because he is infinitely worthy. Whenever God's will is done, something of heaven manifests here on earth. I feel the magnetic pull of God's holiness. I let him change me, and he does—every single day.

Making daily time with God the core of our lives comes with massive benefits. Let's briefly unpack a few, because you won't be able to sustain this discipline without tangible results and blessings along the way.

Interaction. God does who he says he is. When you interact with the Good Shepherd, you get shepherded. When you interact with God as Saviour, you get rescued. When you sit with the Bread of Life, he nourishes your soul. When you submit to him as Lord, he leads you. When you sit at the feet of the Teacher, he teaches you. I could go on for pages like this, but just know that God is waiting to meet every issue you face with a specific aspect of his perfect character.

Remembering. Human beings are forgetful creatures. We quickly lose sight of what matters and fixate on what doesn't. It's far too easy to forget what Jesus has done for us. We live as though his death and resurrection aren't the greatest victories ever won. We make decisions like his wisdom isn't available, handle difficulties as though he's on vacation, and wrestle with fears like his promises don't exist. All of us need daily reminders of who God is, who we are, and what's at stake with God's kingdom around us. Daily devotions help you remember what matters most in your life.

Anchoring. Your heart drifts like a rowboat at sea unless it's anchored to something solid. The world around us is maddeningly fluid, changing and shifting like waves. Without daily and intentional anchoring to the God who doesn't change, we'll get sucked into the sea of relativism. Our faith will shatter on the cunning reefs designed by the Enemy to sink our trust in our good Father. It's a marvellous gift to rest secure in his arms while the world goes mad around us.

Processing. Spending time with God every day helps us gain God's perspective on tough conversations, ongoing hardships, unhealthy patterns, worthwhile progress and celebrations, and lessons to learn from every aspect of life. Processing your life as one seated with God is more powerful than you can imagine. Prayer journalling helps us reflect on our growth. I believe it more than doubles the ongoing impact of my personal time with God.

Basking. Your heart longs for the presence of God, and it cannot be satisfied without it. David wrote that "You make known to me the path of life; in your presence there is fullness of joy" (Psalm 16:11), and Peter promised that "times of refreshing may come from the presence of the Lord" (Acts 3:19, NASB). If you don't spend time immersed in God's glory, you're going to seek substitute glory somewhere else. Actually, if you aren't regularly spending time in God's presence, you are already seeking a substitute somewhere else.

It's time to tackle the last paradigm shift you need to embrace in order to go deep with Jesus.

Key points from this chapter:

• A Quiet Time (or Daily Devotions) is a regular block of time set apart for personal interaction with God.

• *The Father's goal* for your quiet times is to deepen your relationship so he can have you for himself.

• Your goal should be to give yourself more fully to God. A 'successful' devotional time isn't just one where I get something out of God; it's where God gets something out of me.

• **Q:** *Has your goal for spending time with God been to give yourself more fully to him, or has it been something else? How do you think that affected your experience with God?*

• Our daily devotions are the place where we can give God our full attention, our deepest affection, our dependence, and our obedience.

• Truth by truth, lie by lie, value by value, we gradually learn to walk in God's ways and become more like Jesus.

• **Q:** *Are you becoming more like Jesus over time, or remaining basically the same? Why do you think that is?*

• There are life-changing benefits reaped by spending time with God every day—like interaction, remembering, anchoring, processing, and basking.

• **Q:** *Which of these benefits do you currently experience in your daily time with God? Which would you love to experience more of, and why?*

4

Shift Three: Ownership

A few days before Mother's Day rolled around one year, I pulled two lonely racks of ribs from the freezer and let them thaw overnight to prepare for my bride's enjoyment. She's a self-described carnivore who also eats salad, but that's another story.

The next morning, I massaged the meaty pair with a glorious dry rub so they could marinate for twenty-four hours. The next day, I baked them on low heat for several more hours, babying them as the flesh let go of the bone. In the final stretch, I threw them on the BBQ to sear the bark to finger-dripping perfection. Let me tell you, that was a tender, flavour-filled feast we all enjoyed.

I think I did a pretty good job of describing those ribs for you just now. You can almost taste them, right? Almost. Your mind flirted with some great metaphors. But me? I filled my belly with the actual ribs. Perhaps my culinary frontier has inspired you to attempt some dry ribs of your own. If not, you'll have to settle for thinking about my experience instead of relishing your own meal.

I hope you see where this is going. The Bible compares the word of God (and our interaction with God) to great food—like bread and meat (Hebrews 5:12,13). When I receive revelation from Jesus and his word that feeds my heart, it's a feast fit for a king. Some of these meals take days, weeks, or even months to fully digest and enjoy.

Sometimes my spiritual meals are so life-changing that I want to share them with others. Most of the 1,500+ sermons I've preached over the years grew organically from my time with Jesus. Preaching, teaching, and learning from others is biblical, necessary, and noble. I also think I'm pretty good at it. But spiritually speaking, when you listen to my sermon, *you're eating food I've already chewed.*

The Apostle Paul said truth packaged for immature believers is like mother's milk (I Corinthians 3:1,2). Mother's milk is food that an adult has already processed, then repurposed for an infant who can't yet chew or digest food for themselves. There are definitely nutrients preserved and passed along through pre-chewed food, but the joy of biting into a succulent rib, pulling that glorious meat off the bone, and experiencing the magnum opus of fat-infused flavour? That's reserved for the original eater.

It's strange: There is no "pre-chewed food" section for adults in our supermarkets. No pre-chewed steaks, no partly digested cereals, no chocolate-covered almonds with the chocolate sucked off. Do you know why? No one is looking for pre-chewed food. Or asking for it. Or craving it, or buying it. *Well, of course not,* you're thinking. *That's disgusting.*

A few years ago I hopped into Amazon and typed "Devotional Books" into the search bar—pre-digested, time-released spiritual food— and BOOM! I found numbers 1-16 of more than one hundred thousand book results. It's all there: devotional books for men. For women. Teens. Moms. Girls. Boys. Hamsters going through menopause. A pre-chewed biblical cornucopia for people of all ages.

Hmmm. So then I searched, "How to do daily devotions," and just two-hundred and forty-five results popped up—*in total*—none of which show people how to do daily devotions. So I tried, "How to have a daily quiet time" and got seven results, none of which showed me how to have a quiet time. One listing was for a blow dryer. Another was for an electric egg cooker-boiler, which is cool—but didn't help me with my daily quiet time. On Amazon, at least, there is almost zero demand for a book that teaches people how to spend time with God every day. Let that sink in.

Reading cultivated truth-bites other people have written is not enough. A diet of pre-chewed food stunts our faith development. Devotional workbooks are far better, since they engage readers in the learning process and help them discover truths on their own. But even then, the focus is the 'learning' part of intimacy with God, as if that's all that matters. I've never seen a devotional book that helps a reader engage in a full spectrum of spiritual activities ...until now.

The framework I'm going to teach you will help you incorporate venting, prayer, thanksgiving, praise, confession, repentance, receiving God's affirmation, declaration, listening to God's word and Spirit, Spirit-led prayer, and worship into your daily quiet time.

If you're a "devotional book person," you may feel judged or criticized right now. Please don't. We all need to learn from others. But to enjoy a rich and life-changing quiet time, you'll have to break your dependence on devotional books, mobile apps, or blog posts so you can learn to experience God for yourself. I truly believe you can do it. In fact, I believe in you *more than you believe in yourself.*

If you've picked up this book, congratulations! You're not content with spoon-fed truth. You have a desire to learn a skill very few others have an interest in acquiring. Seriously, that desire is a big deal. God has been waiting for you to do something about it.

Maybe you're reading a really good devotional. I've written one myself! But as writer, teacher, and poet Jackie Hill Perry says, "This is an appetizer. This is guacamole and chips, but Jesus is the bread." I'd like you to take the devotional book you're working through... and set it aside until you've learned how to draw from Jesus yourself. Get out your Bible, some paper, and a nice pen. If you feel intimidated by the thought of doing this yourself, the ancient Hebrews are going to help you leave that fear in the rear-view mirror.

Thousands of years ago, the Israelites found themselves freshly emancipated from their crushing captivity in Egypt. Soon afterwards, they got to meet the God who had just delivered them from the most powerful nation on earth. Moses, their God-appointed leader, had just descended from the mountaintop with ten commandments in hand, hot off the Sinai press. And then—try to picture this now—God himself stepped out of the invisible realm to introduce himself:

> "On the morning of the third day there was thunder and lightning, with a thick cloud over the mountain, and a very loud trumpet blast. Everyone in the camp trembled.
>
> Then Moses led the people out of the camp to meet with God, and they stood at the foot of the mountain. Mount Sinai was covered with smoke, because the Lord descended on it in fire. The smoke billowed up from it like smoke from a furnace, and the whole mountain trembled violently. As the sound of the trumpet grew louder and louder, Moses spoke and the voice of God answered him" (Exodus 20:16-20).

The Israelites trembled in awe, as we all would! Next, the God of the universe walked them through the ten commandments—aloud—to make sure they got the point (20:1-17). What a fantastic moment. Picture meeting God, right before your eyes. Imagine God reading his word aloud to you! That's what we want, right? To experience God more deeply and profoundly? Unfortunately, the humans present that day—the ones standing there as proxy for us all, totally bailed:

"When the people saw the thunder and lightning and heard the trumpet and saw the mountain in smoke, they trembled with fear. They stayed at a distance and said to Moses, "Speak to us yourself and we will listen. But do not have God speak to us or we will die." ...The people remained at a distance, while Moses approached the thick darkness where God was" (Exodus 20:18,19,21)

Translation? Here is how I read it:

"Mmmkay. You do the *thing*, Moses. You do the talking to God, because wow—you've clearly got a hotline to heaven. That, and we find God a bit much. Tell you what... how about you just go up the mountain and come back down to tell us what God told you?"

If this happened today, the story might take a slightly different flavour:

"Hey, pastor/writer/blogger/super-Christian! You clearly have a hotline to heaven, because you see stuff in the Bible I could never have come up with in a million years. I find all that Bible study stuff intimidating, TBH.

Here's what I'm thinking: you could take what God teaches you in your daily devotions, write it down for the rest of us, and then we can read your words every day instead of listening directly to God. While you're at it, break the material into 365 chunks so I can drink in maybe nine minutes per day—you know, pre-chewed, bite-sized nuggets of godly goodness. With a prayer at the end, please and thank-you."

To be clear, I read Christian books regularly. I've even worked through a few devotional books. There's nothing wrong with them, per se. It is wrong, however, to make devotional books the backbone of our relationship with God. When we take someone else's 'gently used' relationship with Jesus and try to make it fit like a new sweater, a sense of distance and disappointment is inevitable. Why? Because we're not relating to God ourselves—we're "trying on" a stranger's victories and defeats as if they were our own. They're not.

I also know that for many people, Bible Study, listening to God, prayer journalling, spiritual warfare, confession, worship, and intimacy with God seem like *Christianity: level Expert.* Building your own devotional time with God may feel intimidating, a lot like Moses solo-climbing Mount Sinai to venture into the thick, mysterious darkness where God was.

I've written this book as a field guide that will help you explore the wild and beautiful places God wants you to venture into. This is not the only way to spend time with God, though it is a biblically ordained, heaven-blessed way that helps you interact meaningfully with Jesus every single day. I'm going to show you *how*; you'll have to take the time to invest in your own relationship with God. If you do, your adventure with God will take you places you've never been before.

Jesus didn't launch his revolution by deploying super-squads of seminary grads. He began with un-ejumuh-cated knuckleheads who made him face-palm repeatedly. So you can do this. You can learn to connect with him for yourself, learn how to study the Bible, hear God's voice, experience the filling of his Spirit, and revel in the presence of God.

Take a few minutes to confess that intimidation. Invite Jesus into it. Ask him what he'd like you to know about your insecurity. You, my friend, are a child of God. Your Father is the King of all Kings. You've got this, because he's got you.

The good news is, once you run with these three paradigm shifts—responding to God's initiative, setting biblical relationship goals, and taking ownership of your part of that relationship—the pathway towards victory is going to feel a lot more like gliding down a hill on your bike than peddling up a mountain.

Let's get started.

Key points from this chapter:

- When our spiritual growth depends on devotional books, this diet of pre-chewed food stunts our spiritual growth.

- **Q:** *If you're a 'devotional book person,' did you feel yourself becoming defensive while reading this chapter? If so, why?*

- It's normal to feel intimidated by a relational approach to daily devotions, but our intimacy with God depends on it.

- This book is like a 'field guide' that will train you in nine key spiritual practices. God will meet you and empower you for the journey!

- You can learn to connect with Jesus for yourself. You can learn how to study the Bible. You can learn to hear God's voice, experience the filling of the Spirit, and revel in the presence of God.

- **Q:** *Do you believe God can teach you how to connect with him yourself and grow a world-changing intimacy with Jesus? Why or why not?*

- **Pray:** *Ask Jesus to help you overcome your doubts and train you, like he did with his original twelve disciples!*

Part Two:
The Temple Pathway

5

The Power of God's Path

"The Lord God formed a man from the dust of the ground and breathed into his nostrils the breath of life, and the man became a living being.

Now the Lord God had planted a garden in the east, in Eden; and there he put the man he had formed." (Genesis 2:7,8)

If you take a fish out of water, it will die. A palm tree planted in Alaska won't make it past October. You can start a grapevine in central Canada, but it will never produce a bumper crop. Why? Because living things require specific environments to thrive.

The opening chapters of Genesis inform us that *the garden of Eden is our natural habitat.* God created us for Eden, and he created Eden for us. Life is hard, in part, because we're not living there anymore.

In the beginning, Eden was a place of wonder, freedom, and delight. The garden was the ecstatic expression of God's perfect shalom, the ideal environment for human joy and thriving. Adam and Eve were perfectly right with God, perfectly right with each other, perfectly right with their world. All they knew was peace. Joy. Communion. Delight.

Outside the garden, the world was untamed outback, awaiting God's imagers to go to work on it. God's plan was simple: "God blessed them and said to them, "Be fruitful and increase in number; fill the earth and subdue it." (Genesis 1:28). Translation: *As you multiply, your offspring will spread across the earth, slowly turning the outback into Eden.*

What a glorious mission!

But then. Oh, the tragedy bleeding from those two words!

When Adam and Eve obeyed the tempter, the world broke. And they did, too. Everything that was so exquisitely right went horribly wrong: Shame. Blame. Fear. Deception. Separation. Stress. Division. Stress. Pain. Worst of all, their unbroken fellowship with God broke too:

> "The man and his wife heard the sound of the Lord God as he was walking in the garden in the cool of the day, and they hid from the Lord God among the trees of the garden. But the Lord God called to the man, "Where are you?" (Genesis 3:8,9)

This haunts me. It hurts my heart. "You had it, Adam," I want to shout. "You had a perfect intimacy with God, and you threw it away!" Of course, we've all been doing that ever since. But that day, Adam and Eve went their own way, and the consequences were gut-wrenching:

> "The Lord God banished him from the Garden of Eden to work the ground from which he had been taken. After he drove the man out, he placed on the east side of the Garden of Eden cherubim and a flaming sword flashing back and forth to guard the way to the tree of life." (Genesis 3:23,24).

From that day forward, we've been living outside of Eden, trying to find our way back in. When that doesn't work, we settle for less—so much less.

It didn't take us long to defile everything God had made. Just three chapters later, in Genesis chapter six, we read, "God saw how corrupt the earth had become, for all the people on earth had corrupted their *ways*" (Genesis 6:12). They weren't just doing bad things. Their *ways* had become corrupt, which sped up and amplified sin's corrupting power.

What's a 'way?' The dictionary tells us a way is "a method, style or manner of doing something." A second sense of the word refers to "a road or path for travelling along." Biblically, our ways refer to the life-paths created by how we think, speak, and act—including where those pathways are leading us. Simply put, *a way* is a *how*.

Since the days of Noah, one of the common themes of scripture is that we need to "turn from (our) wicked ways" (II Chronicles 7:14) and learn to walk in God's ways instead. My ways, even if they seem right to me, end in death (Proverbs 16:25). They corrupt the world and make things worse. God's ways, in contrast, are the path of life. In the broadest sense, they lead us back into Eden.

Let that sink in: God has ways. And his wake-up call is this: "My thoughts are not your thoughts, neither are my ways your ways," (Isaiah 55:8,9). Our ways are utterly corrupt. His ways are perfectly pure.

This is why David prayed, "Search me, God, and know my heart; test me and know my anxious thoughts. See if there is any offensive *way* in me, and lead me in the *way* everlasting" (Psalm 139:23,24).

As I already mentioned, "Moses used to take a tent and pitch it outside the camp some distance away, calling it the 'tent of meeting.'... where "The LORD would speak with Moses face to face, as a man speaks with his friend" (Exodus 33:7,11). This is where Moses prayed, "Teach me your *ways* so that I may know you and continue to find favour with you" (Exodus 33:11,13).

In his regular FaceTime with the Almighty, Moses observed that even the unfathomable God of the universe, sovereign and uncontainable as he is, operates with discernible patterns. And learning those ways, Moses realized, is a key factor in getting to know God himself! He also understood what we often miss: The key to life is learning to walk in God's ways, not expecting God to conform to ours.

This just makes sense. If a guy is crushing on a girl and she frequents Starbucks each morning, he's much more likely to connect with her if he hangs out there, too. And you're much more likely to "bump into God" —to experience him—when you walk in his ways as a way of life.

I can understand Moses' request for a greater revelation of God's ways. For a dozen chapters (Exodus 20-32) God laid out the ten commandments and the basic framework for what would become the tabernacle and priesthood in Israel. It must have made Moses' head spin. "What's your intention with all of this?" he seemed to wonder.

After Moses' "Show me your ways" prayer, God spent the rest of the book of Exodus answering him. To begin with, he expanded on Moses' simplistic "tent of meeting" concept. The symbolism of the tabernacle must have made Moses' jaw drop. It:

- Was an oasis of divine design, set up in the wilderness
- Included a tree of life/knowledge
- Displayed cherubim on the curtains, restricting general access
- Depicted the consequences of sin, how that affects our relationship with God, and what God would have to accomplish in Christ to fix it.

The elements and design of the tabernacle mirror every major element found in Eden. The message is obvious: God is showing us the way back into Eden and providing a pathway to go there.

God also shared detailed construction blueprints for the tabernacle with Moses. These blueprints held an intentional 'floor plan' which guided the priests through a God-ordained flow of worship. This pathway culminated with the high priest entering the Holy of Holies to meet face to face with God.

When the Hebrews completed the construction of the tabernacle, it was time to begin a new era of communing with their Deliverer. The book of Exodus closes with this incredible verse: "Then the cloud covered the Tent of Meeting, and the glory of the LORD filled the tabernacle" (Exodus 40:34).

God visibly blessed the tabernacle structure as a heavenly *how-to*—the official "way" he would interact with his people on earth. God was saying, "Yes. Like this. Do it like this." Each space within the floor plan guided people through his courts with life-changing practices or disciplines that taught people *how to walk in God's ways.* The 'tent of meeting' didn't just facilitate public worship; it showed people how to approach God.

Generations later, the Hebrews had established themselves in the promised land of Israel. God instructed them to build a permanent stonework Temple there. The Lord laid out this mammoth wonder with the same blueprint as the tabernacle in order to accomplish the same purpose. It provided a special place where the people could meet and interact with him, and it showed them—step-by-step, no less—exactly how to do it. The message was clear: "If you want to connect with me, this is how it works."

The prophet Isaiah prophesied, "Many peoples will come and say, "Come, let us come and go up to the mountain of the Lord, *to the temple* of the God of Jacob. He will teach us his *ways*, so that we may walk in his paths" (Isaiah 2:3). I need to say it again: *the Temple Pathway is a flow of worship designed to teach us to walk in God's ways.*

During the Temple era, King David penned Psalm 84, one of my favourites. Notice all the Temple imagery:

"How lovely is your dwelling place, Lord Almighty! My soul yearns, even faints, for the courts of the Lord; my heart and my flesh cry out for the living God.

Even the sparrow has found a home, and the swallow a nest for herself, where she may have her young—a place near your altar, Lord Almighty, my King and my God. Blessed are those who dwell in your house; they are ever praising you.

Blessed are those whose strength is in you, whose hearts are set on pilgrimage." (Psalm 84:1-5).

The best translation of this last verse is, "Blessed is the man whose strength is in Thee, *in whose heart are Thy ways*" (Psalm 84:5, KJV21). This is beautiful! My ways begin corrupt, leading me away from God instead of toward him. But as God shows me his ways, I repent of them so I can learn to walk in his paths. Over time, what feels foreign to me becomes natural. God's ways become engraved on my heart.

When this happens, it's not just that I'm walking in God's ways. We're walking them *together*. We've returned to the very heartbeat of Eden. Learning God's ways, like everything else, is about deepening our intimacy with Jesus and walking with him.

So... you're up bright and early, with an open Bible before you. Your regular devotional book is off the table, and you're cradling a steaming hot coffee instead. You've got eighteen minutes set aside to spend interacting with God. Now what? Has anyone ever taught you how to do that?

I used to believe the Bible had nothing to say about how to spend my "God-time." It was up to me, or so I thought, to figure out daily devotions. Beyond a few vague biblical principles and guardrails, intimacy with God was a 'choose your own adventure' kind of thing.

Now I see what was hiding in plain sight—a clear and powerful pathway designed by God to help us grow our intimacy with him.

I'm not saying The Temple Pathway is the only right way to 'do your devotions.' And I'm definitely not a rule guy. I hate being put into boxes. I can't stand working within constraints that hamper my autonomy and creativity. So believe me when I tell you that the pathway outlined in this book won't box you in. It will set you free. That, and we need structure to survive.

In the beginning, the Spirit of God hovered over chaotic darkness and spoke light and order into the confusion. Next, he set clear boundaries for entire categories of matter: sea and land, earth and sky, light and darkness, male and female, night and day. For all of creation's mind-boggling complexity and randomness, there is a breathtaking order to her form. The true genius of our universe's design lies not in its terrifying vastness, but in its elegant and intimate structures. The cosmos is a fractal kaleidoscope of patterns within patterns that make all life, progress, and science possible.

Civilization itself is the fruit of humanity's imposing structure on nature as we "fill the earth and subdue it" (Genesis 1:28). Language, celebrations, work weeks, Evernote apps, calendars, neighbourhoods, school zones, marriage certificates, area codes, curriculum—these are all important forms of structure. And while it's true that too much structure suffocates us, too little structure immobilizes us. Without structure, we're pathetic blobs of tissue and tendon, crying out for a skeleton to give us form.

God's Temple Pathway gives us this life-giving structure. Within the flow of the Temple, we can learn the rhythms of grace and gospel. We're guided through five important spaces: *Ascent, the Gates & Outer Court, the Court of Priests, the Holy Place, and the Holy of Holies.*

Each of these spaces become vital parts of our daily devotional pathway. I'll explain each of them briefly, then spend full chapters unpacking the power of each in turn.

Ascent

God's Temple was located within Jerusalem, a walled city perched on a giant hill. Pilgrims from all over the Judean countryside routinely converged on the city to worship, offer sacrifices, and enjoy a rich variety of faith festivals. Because of where the city was located, the pilgrimage to Jerusalem involved a literal ascent as they trudged up a hill to get there.

Pilgrims used their physical ascent to engage in a kind of spiritual ascent as well. As they approached the city, they reflected on what was on their minds and give it over to God in prayer. Groups who travelled together used an inspired songbook (found in Psalms 120 through 134) to help them focus their hearts and minds as they ascended towards the Temple.

Gates and Outer Court

When the worshippers reached the city, things got complicated. Anyone could enter the outer Temple complex, but strict rules forbade women, children, and Gentiles from going further in. Jewish men in good standing could ascend several grand stairs as they passed through massive gates to enter the outer courts. Overjoyed to be in the temple, they thanked God for what he'd done for them and praised him for who he is.

The Court of Priests

Only the priests and Levites could ascend a second set of stairs to pass from the outer courts "further up and further in" to the Temple area, where the Court of Priests was located. This zone functioned as a killing floor where priests sacrificed animals to God to atone for the sins of the people. A giant laver (a bronze basin of water) also stood ready, where the priests washed their hands to rid themselves of the blood and gore.

The Holy Place

Beyond the Court of Priests, another set of stairs led the way through a doorway that took priests inside the Temple building itself to enter the Holy Place. The Holy Place housed three important pieces of furniture:

- An ornate table with twelve fresh loaves of bread on top
- A golden, seven-pronged lampstand, perpetually lit
- An altar for burning incense as an offering to God.

The sacrifices made in the Court of Priests made the activities and equipment of the Holy Place holy and acceptable to God.

The Holy of Holies

On the far wall of the Holy Place, a final set of stairs leads to a six-inch-thick, beautifully embroidered curtain. Behind the curtain lay the mysterious heart of the Temple, the Holy of Holies. This room was permanently sealed off because it housed the legendary Ark of the Covenant. God himself would manifest his glory between two gold sculpted cherubim flanking the heavy cover of the ark.

Only the High Priest could enter the Holy of Holies, just once per year, and only after they had made the proper sacrifices and preparations in the proper order. Even then, fellow priests often fastened a rope around his ankle just in case he made a mistake and God struck him dead. That way they could drag his body back out without sending someone else in to die.

What about Jesus?

You might mention that everything I've explained so far can be found in the Old Testament. And that's true. You might also remind me that Jesus fulfilled the whole Temple system as the promised Messiah. And you'd be absolutely correct! But the pathway is still active in the New Testament as well. In fact, elements of the tabernacle and temple are present from Genesis through the book of Revelation.

After Christ's death and resurrection, the book of Hebrews spends several chapters explaining what Christ accomplished and how that affects how we approach God. Guess what's at the heart of that discussion? The Temple Pathway. After reviewing the Temple structure and flow we've just been talking about in Hebrews 9:1-10, he says,

> "When Christ came as the high priest of the things that are already here, he went through the greater and more perfect tabernacle that is not man-made, that is to say, not a part of this creation. He did not enter by the means of the blood of goats and calves, but entered the Most Holy Place once for all by his own blood, having obtained eternal redemption." (Hebrews 9:11,12).

Did you catch that? God patterned the earthly tabernacle and temple after a spiritual, heavenly tabernacle. Like Hebrews 10:1 says, "The law is only a shadow of the good things that are coming—not the realities themselves." The scriptures clarify that the spiritual and heavenly are far more real than the physical world we take for granted.

Also notice that Jesus, the pioneer and perfecter of our faith himself, used the heavenly Temple Pathway to fulfill his promises to us (Hebrews 12:2). It's that important. But Jesus' fulfillment of the pathway didn't make it obsolete. He *full*-filled it! His victory infused it with even more life, power, and purpose. He "has made us to be a kingdom and priests to serve his God and Father" (Revelation 1:6). As priests, we have access to the Temple and everything it entails.

> "Therefore, brothers, since we have confidence to enter the most Holy Place by the blood of Jesus, *by a new and living way* opened for us through the curtain, that is, his body, and since we have a great high priest over the house of God, let us draw near to God with a sincere heart in full assurance of faith, having our hearts sprinkled to cleanse us from a guilty conscience and having our bodies washed with pure water. Let us hold unswervingly to the hope we profess, for he who promised is faithful" (Hebrews 10:18-22, *emphasis mine*).

The Temple Pathway has found its full expression in the gospel of Jesus. God wants to help us "draw near" to him through this new and living *way* opened up for us through his Son. This flow of worship was created, travelled, fulfilled and blessed by Christ himself. It is now graced with resurrection life and power because of his work on the cross. The Temple Pathway is now everything God designed it to be—a living way—and as a living way, *it still stands open for you and me.*

In Christ, the old songbook becomes a springboard. The sacrifices offered *by* us are replaced by Christ's sacrifice *for* us. The physical place becomes a spiritual posture. The old hoops to jump through become helps that satisfy the deepest needs of our souls. The symbols take on substance. The Ark of the Covenant is the throne of grace (Hebrews 4:16).

Incredible, don't you think?

It's true that God is everywhere—that in Christ, we have access to the Father no matter where we are. You should absolutely pray in the car on the way to work, or read your Bible during a five-minute break before getting back to work after lunch. The Holy Spirit can and does speak to us during the busiest times of our lives. He touches and helps us while we're knee-deep in the mucky trenches of real life, in real time. Praise God.

But access doesn't equal intimacy. Just because we can connect with God throughout the day doesn't mean we do. And connecting with God doesn't mean we're connecting meaningfully, or as deeply as he wants us to. You know this. It's probably one reason you're reading this book.

If you want to experience God's love and power every day, you can. He's left the front door ajar and opened the Temple Pathway to guide you into that reality. Scripture says the *way* Jesus inaugurated helps us approach God with a sincere heart in full assurance of faith. I'm confident that if you approach God this way during your quiet time, you'll experience an intimacy with God you've only dreamed of until now.

This pathway doesn't come up just once or twice in the Bible. The Temple Pathway is *everywhere*. It's the central architecture of the biblical narrative.

God met with Moses in a tent of meeting. He elaborated on this approach with the tabernacle. He then underlined it in the Temple. Eventually, Jesus embodied this way through his death and resurrection.

And finally, God reminds us in the book of Hebrews that Christ's living way still stands for us to embrace personally. Think of it: God worked for thousands of years, with millions of people, spending billions of dollars, to give us this powerful model. There is nothing on earth like it.

You might still feel some inward resistance to using this ancient way to approach and experience God. The Temple Pathway opens up four powerful benefits no other approach offers.

1. **The Temple Pathway is gospel-centred.** It shows us how to trust Jesus Christ and His finished work as the foundation for all of life. Each space in the pathway points us to Christ and helps us apply what he's done to every issue we face. This alone will be transformational because it helps us live "in view of God's mercy" (Romans 12:1).

2. **The Temple Pathway teaches us how to grow deep intimacy with God.** Guys, don't worry—intimacy isn't flowery or romantic. It simply describes what we share with someone. This is why intimacy is always mutual:

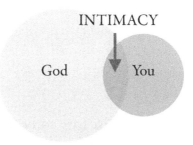

Through the Temple Pathway, God will share his heart with you, and you'll return the favour. Over time, the depth and breadth of what you share with God will increase.

3. **The Temple Pathway trains us in nine key spiritual disciplines or practices.** Yes, *nine!* Each of these practices bring us into greater harmony with God's ways over time.

You'll learn to vent your struggles to God in life-changing ways. You'll build your faith through thanksgiving and the power of praise. You will learn how to come into God's light for a 'heart-check,' confess your sins, and give and receive God's grace. You'll learn how to listen to God and receive his word. You will discover the fruitfulness of Spirit-led prayer, and learn the beauty of basking in God's presence through intimate worship.

All of these practices—and all their incredible benefits—are baked into the pathway. You could also think of these elements as essential ingredients for intimacy and a vibrant spiritual life. Once you learn these nine practices, they'll be instantly accessible to you in any circumstance.

4. **The Temple Pathway helps us process our life experiences so we can become more like Jesus over time.** Through this approach, you'll learn how to process ongoing disappointment, pain, victory, and failure with Jesus. God will help you develop a healthy self-awareness. As you meet him in the pathway, he will guide you into truth. As your heart changes, your life will follow.

It saddens me to think of how many people content themselves with reading something someone else learned, hoping it resonates with their lives that day, praying a pre-fabricated prayer, and then saying amen! Maybe that's your story, too.

The good news is, it doesn't have to be. This book is my way of mentoring you in the Temple Pathway. Each chapter of this book will equip you to go deeper with God and anchor you more richly in the gospel. You'll be trained in those nine spiritual practices, and you will learn how to process your life so you can become more like Jesus.

Once you taste it, you'll never go back.

Yes, the Temple Pathway is for you, no matter what season you're slugging through right now. I'm going to coach you through the entire pathway, step by step. But (spoiler alert!) I'll also show you a "five-minute flow" and a "fifteen-minute flow" in Part Three of this book if you need to start small.

Sound like a plan?

Let's get to it.

Key points from this chapter:

• One of our deepest needs is to turn from our broken ways to learn to walk in God's perfect ways.

• Too much structure in our relationship with God stifles us, but too little structure leaves us without direction or purpose.

• The tabernacle is a heavenly blueprint designed by God to teach us how to engage with God. It didn't just facilitate worship, it showed people how to approach God and walk in his ways.

• God's Temple Pathway includes five important spaces: *Ascent, Gates and Outer Courts, the Court of Priests, the Holy Place, and the Holy of Holies.* Each step is a vital part of our daily time with God.

• Christ has fulfilled the Temple Pathway and filled it with his resurrection life and power. Its become everything it was designed to be—a living way that still stands for you and me.

• If we approach God in God's way during our quiet time, we'll experience a deeper intimacy with God.

• The Temple Pathway is gospel-centred, teaches us how to grow deep intimacy with God, trains us in nine key spiritual practices, and helps us process our journey so we can become more like Jesus over time.

• Q: *What do you think of the truth that to encounter more of God, we need to walk in his ways instead of expecting him to adapt to ours?*

• Q: *Can you see how the Temple Pathway might be useful for connecting with God? Why or why not?*

• Q: *What excites you most about this approach so far? What questions or hesitations do you still have?*

6

Ascent

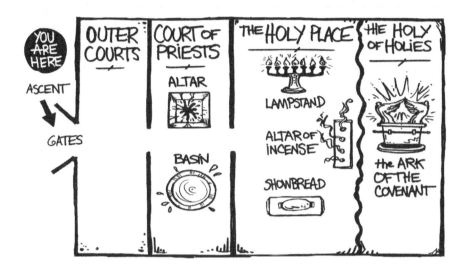

Where should our time with God begin?

Well, the first thing you need to know about spending time with God is this: You get to be yourself.

You're allowed to feel what you feel, wrestle with your issues, vent like a mad-person and be completely honest about the shameful struggles you can't seem to get off your mind. You can cry, laugh, blow off steam, and completely lose it. God wants you to come as you are, wherever your heart happens to be. We actually *need to* be human for our quiet time to become the rich source of life God intended.

Unfortunately, that's not how most people approach their time with God. For most of my life I'd sit down with my Bible and put on my best spiritual attitude and try to connect with God from there. I tried to elevate myself into God's presence by thinking godly thoughts. Quiet time was "holy time."

I think I picked up the habit in church. How many Sunday mornings have you heard a well-meaning pastor or worship leader say, "Okay, welcome here this morning. Let's just lay aside all our struggles now, all our conflict, all our issues. Let's put them down for an hour and focus our eyes on Jesus." And how many times have you tried to do that —attempted to leave your junk at the door so you could meet with God?

It sounds so spiritual, so right. *Jesus is worthy, so get over yourself. It's holy time, people!* This is how the Lord's Prayer seems to begin: "Our Father in heaven, hallowed be your name; your kingdom come, your will be done, on earth as it is in heaven" (Matthew 6:9,10). But Jesus wasn't teaching his disciples to lay aside their cares and worries; the rest of the prayer dives right into them. He was teaching us how to *present ourselves to God* (Romans 12:1,2).

Christ's disciples were already familiar with the Temple Pathway. It was woven into the fabric of their daily lives. In this prayer, Jesus was giving them a deeper understanding of how to draw near as sons of the Father. I can assure you that Jesus was not telling them, "If you want to connect with my Father, you'll need to put on a righteous attitude and drop the cares and worries you're carrying." Like I said, the rest of the Lord's Prayer dives deeply into the stuff we struggle with on a daily basis.

While religion strives to ascend toward God by creating our own holiness, the message of the gospel is that God condescends to us. Jesus "became flesh and dwelt among us" (John 1:14). Paul says Jesus "made himself nothing by taking the very nature of a servant, being made in human likeness. And being found in appearance as a man, he humbled himself by becoming obedient to death—even death on a cross!" (Philippians 2:7,8). God meets you where you're at so he can lift you up to where he is. That's what the gospel does.

Your quiet time doesn't require you to be on your best behaviour. That's religion, not the gospel! Shutting your needs out of your prayer and worship sends the message that your faith has precious little to do with your actual life. But God wants you to be absolutely real so he can meet you in the trenches, where life actually happens.

Regardless of how you think a prayer should begin, please understand: Jesus doesn't want you to drop your junk at the door before coming in. He wants you to drag the whole stinking mess with you into his presence so he can saturate it with his grace and truth. The 'holy time' attitude misses the whole point of having a quiet time—learning to live your whole life deeply in God. It also robs you of the most natural place to start: again, your actual life.

Jesus says, "I am the Vine, and you are the branches. If you abide in me and I abide in you, you will bear much fruit" (John 15:5). To abide means to *live in*, not just to think focused, spiritual thoughts about. "If you live your entire life in me," Jesus is saying, "I will live the fullness of my life through you—and together we'll change the world." Wow!

I think the "holy time" mentality moves people to buy devotional books instead of studying the Bible for themselves. We're hiring people more spiritually-minded than we are to give us more profound spiritual thoughts to think, more spiritual prayers to pray, and a clever spiritual thought we could never come up with ourselves, to guide our day. I read Christian books all the time, but they can't replace one-on-one time with my Lord and Saviour.

If you like devotional books you've probably experienced moments when you thought, "Wow, that's crazy. This is just what I needed today!" It's humbling that the God of the universe would orchestrate things so that a specific devotional entry would hit you where you live, right when you need it. Unfortunately, getting hit between the eyes is going to be rare if you're trying to connect with God using material downloaded from someone else's head space while living a completely different life than yours.

A quiet time that speaks directly to your current experience should never surprise you. Your quiet time is supposed to hit you where you live *every single time*. If you want God to hit you where you live, then where you live is where to begin. So let's talk about the launch pad for your quiet time: *Ascent*.

As Hebrew pilgrims ascended the hill towards the temple in Jerusalem, they reflected on what was on their minds and gave it over to God in prayer. They often used Psalms 120 through 134 like an ancient version of Pinterest or Instagram: an 'idea book' to get them started.

- Psalms 124 and 126 focus on relishing a **God-moment** or **answer to prayer**

- Psalm 128 unpacks **a truth** God has been teaching the writer

- Psalm 129 celebrates **a victory** over a recent struggle

- Psalm 120 walks through **a current problem** weighing on the writer's heart

- Psalms 121, 125, and 127 start with **a metaphor** for our walk with God and unpack the implications

- Psalm 123 and 131 unpack **relational images** (master/slave, mother/child) in prayer

- Psalm 130 unravels **a fresh sin** the writer committed, including how they feel about it

If you need some help with your *Ascent*, try a few of these biblical springboards and you'll be swimming in the deep end in no time. That said, the "Psalms of Ascent" list isn't exhaustive. The Holy Spirit will help you express what's on your heart. You might try starting your quiet time with these gems:

Complaints. I'm serious. If you don't grumble *to* God, you'll just end up grumbling *against* God. The former is welcomed as part of the conversation (Psalm 142:1,2; John 6:61). The latter is a sin (Numbers 14:27). King David lodges countless complaints to God throughout the Psalms.

Frustration and anger. Tell God when your life doesn't feel fair, or when circumstances aren't working out like you thought they would. Or when people are being stupid and hurtful. Or even when you're mad at God (Jeremiah 4:10). He already knows, of course, but he wants to talk to you about it. Vent your emotions, using your words—not into the thin air, not just into a punching bag, but to God. He can take it! "Cast your cares on him," Peter says, "Because he cares for you" (I Peter 5:7). *Casting* means throwing. Flinging. Hurling. You get the idea. God catches everything!

Physical pain, sickness, or other struggles. Like your chronic migraines. The flu going around. Your aching back. Your lousy sleep last night. I can tell you from experience, this list will get longer as you get older, and that's okay.

Fears, worries, and anxiety (Philippians 4:6,7). This includes the critical meeting you've been obsessing about. What the lump on your shoulder might be made of. Whether the new couple will like you. Whether you'll get everything done around the house this weekend. The self-doubt you feel when you pray about sharing your faith with a co-worker.

Questions, confusion, and doubts. The Psalms record hundreds of questions, doubts, and confusing moments for the writers. Remember how patient the resurrected Jesus was with 'doubting' Thomas. The poor guy had been wondering whether Jesus had risen from the dead. Doubts and questions don't have to undermine our faith. Giving our questions to God helps us "doubt our doubts" as someone has said. I love that.

Temptations. Like the co-worker you feel drawn to. The internet site you shouldn't visit again. The last piece of cake in the fridge. Your habit of driving by the gym instead of going inside, or not spending time with God regularly. Jesus modelled praying through temptation in the garden of Gethsemane.

Desires. On several occasions, Jesus asked people, "What do you want?" (Matthew 20:32, Mark 10:36, 51). This isn't because God wants to give us everything we want. It's because our desires are often twisted and deceitful, and God wants to heal and transform our desires to resonate with his (Ephesians 4:22-24). We begin by admitting we have them.

The great thing with *Ascent* is, nothing is off limits. If you're going to live your entire life saturated by God, you need to bring your entire life to God. The Father heals and fills whatever we give him.

A friend of mine once tried this Temple Pathway idea for her quiet time. She told me that her brain kept channel surfing during her *Ascent*: "And this, and this, and that, and that, and the other thing..." She was concerned that she'd never get to the end of the venting session because so many things kept popping into her mind. Maybe you can relate to her experience.

Don't worry; you're not infinite, so you'll exhaust yourself eventually. The reason you have a hundred and forty-two things on your list is you've let them accumulate without processing them. They're like a giant pile of leaves in your brain. Every time you open the door to God, the wind of his Spirit swirls them into a crazy mess. If you raked up your stray thoughts and bagged them with God every day, there wouldn't be so many to deal with at one time. You'd probably have three or four, maybe half-a-dozen at the most.

The truth is, those things matter to God anyway. This paradigm shift is profound: Those stupid things that keep popping into your mind aren't distractions; they're the point. When Jesus interacted with people, their real-time struggles and experiences *became the curriculum.* The same is true for you. What's on your mind is an important part of your journey with God.

You might protest: "Most of the things on my mind aren't very spiritual." No, they're probably not. At least some of it is embarrassing or petty. But it's real, so sharing these things with God is vital. Remember, too, that our *Ascent* is just the launch pad for deeper moments. We won't stay there for long. God meets us where we are so he can take us where he is. We learn to go "higher up and further in," to borrow a phrase from the Chronicles of Narnia.

Spoiler alert: your life isn't about you, it's about Jesus. One of the most pressing needs you have is to get over yourself. And you will, if you go with the flow of the Temple Pathway. It's just that the only way to get over yourself is to give yourself to him—all of yourself.

Starting with what's already eating you alive is practical. It's on your mind, anyway! God knows that, and he'd rather help you get it off your chest than pretend it isn't there and fight against it the whole time you're together.

C.S. Lewis also once said, "May it be the real I who speaks. May it be the real Thou that I speak to." Unspooling your tangled reality is the first (and non-negotiable) step towards giving everything to God and living your entire existence saturated with who he is. If you don't start by being real, how can you expect a genuine experience with him?

What's at stake?

You may not sense it, but the entire trajectory of your life hangs in the balance. Let me remind you why it's so important to build intimacy with God every day.

This morning, the Holy Spirit reminded me of the words he spoke to Cain—the very first murderer. Cain and Abel were brothers, the offspring of Adam and Eve. Their chilling story unfolds in Genesis chapter four, when the pair presents their offerings to the Lord. God looked with favour on Abel's offering, but did not approve of Cain's gift. "So Cain was very angry, and his face was downcast" (Genesis 4:5).

We've all felt angry, frustrated, or downcast. Let's add confused, helpless, hopeless, rejected, guilty, ashamed, and a hundred other emotional struggles to this list. Notice what God did next for Cain:

> "Then the Lord said to Cain, "Why are you angry? Why is your face downcast? If you do what is right, will you not be accepted? But if you do not do what is right, sin is crouching at your door; it desires to have you, but you must rule over it" (Genesis 5:6,7).

God pulled Cain aside to offer him several merciful (though terrifying) insights.

1. There is a battle going on for your soul. Sin wants to have you, to own you. It's waiting to see what you do with your anger.

2. If you don't process the negative emotions swirling inside you, sin will take possession of you and ruin you.

3. God gives Cain a command: *You must rule over sin, not the other way around.*

Don't miss this: How we process our struggles determines which master we end up serving. Cain ignored God's advice. He didn't process his anger and jealousy with God. And "sin, seizing the opportunity afforded by the commandment, produced in (him) every kind of coveting" (Romans 7:8)—and far, far worse. Cain, as the story goes, murdered his brother and left him to rot.

Cain didn't realize it, but rejecting God's invitation to process his anger was a decision to destroy his future. The Father initiated a personal conversation with Cain that apparently made him uncomfortable.

Unclenching his fists to talk to God would have opened a window of intimacy, freedom, and victory, but Cain chose to 'handle it' on his own.

We need to spend time with God every day, too. It's the only way to process our struggles, wounds, and emotions so they don't morph into destructive choices and behaviours. King David faced the same sin crouching at his door. He also sensed God's divine invitation to intimacy and a better path. He penned the famous Psalm 23 in response:

> "The Lord is my shepherd, I lack nothing.
>
> He makes me lie down in green pastures, he leads me beside quiet waters, he refreshes my soul.
> He guides me along the right paths for his name's sake.
>
> Even though I walk through the darkest valley,
> I will fear no evil, for you are with me; your rod and your staff, they comfort me.
>
> You prepare a table before me in the presence of my enemies. You anoint my head with oil; my cup overflows.
>
> Surely your goodness and love will follow me all the days of my life, and I will dwell in the house of the Lord forever."

Left to ourselves, we drift towards self-destruction. The only way to walk the pathway of life and grace is to embrace the gospel. Our only hope is to centre our lives around what Jesus has done for us and what the Holy Spirit can do in us. We must learn to plant our lives in the presence of God, full stop. He will address what needs addressing and help us process our struggles in such a way that we rule over sin instead of being mastered by it.

Friend, God's path of life is built on him. We must spend time alone with the Father, Son, and Holy Spirit every day. Sin is crouching at our door. It wants to have us. The best-case scenario when we reject God's call is a lesser life. The worst-case scenario, which absolutely may happen to you, is a life of bondage and death.

Some practical advice with *Ascent*: Be specific enough with your venting that you feel a weight off your chest for sharing, and brief enough that you don't get stuck in the mud. I highly recommend writing this down. Bullet points are probably specific enough, or you may start going in circles:

- I didn't sleep well. So tired. Concerned about my workday now.
- Wondering if I should talk to Bob today...
- I really want to be more aware of your presence today. Help!
- This weekend the fam is coming over. Should be fun!

If you are processing profound grief or trauma, bullet points won't be enough. In that case, I would recommend taking Solomon's advice: "Pour out your heart like water in the presence of the Lord" (Lamentations 2:19). Pray and write until you've given full expression to what's on your heart. Bring it to God every day for as long as it takes. Your sadness and wounds are important to him.

A word of caution: During your *Ascent* you're being real, but that doesn't mean your thinking is sound. Processing your issues in your current headspace would probably just feed your flesh. The focus of the *Ascent* phase is moving your thoughts and feelings from introspection to prayer—presenting them to God—but don't make them prayer *requests* yet. Your emotions tell you what you believe, not what's true. Feelings make a great thermometer, but a lousy compass.

A prayer request involves asking God to resolve the issues you're facing in a specific way. Many times, you've already got some pretty clear ideas about that: "Dear Lord, please cause my idiot boss to get hit by a blimp," which may or may not be God's best for you (or for your boss).

Writing down the issue and bringing it with you as you move through the rest of the Pathway gives God space to work on you before you pray about it. He will peel back the layers of your heart to expose what's really going on: *Perhaps wanting your boss to die a horrible death won't solve your problem; perhaps that anger says something important about your heart.* And don't worry—you'll come back to all the stuff you've logged later on, in the *Holy Place*, when you're tracking better with God and his purposes for you.

A friend of mine once tried to put this Temple Pathway concept into action during his quiet time. I say *tried* because he started twice but never got farther than *Ascent*. Life happens, right? He was eager to go "higher up and further in" the following week, but he said it still felt amazing to pour out all the stuff splashing around in his brain in the presence of God. Even though he didn't get any further than *Ascent*, he was still thrilled to experience God that week.

Like my friend, though, you're ready for the next step.

Key points from this chapter:

• God wants you to be transparent with your actual life, so he can meet you in the trenches, where life actually happens.

• **Q:** *Have you ever brought the 'holy time' mentality into your daily devotions? How has this chapter helped you reframe that approach?*

• Our distractions aren't the enemy. They matter to God, and he wants to talk about them. That's why they're coming up.

• If we don't process our struggles with God, we open the door to sin and bondage long term.

• **Q:** *Has it ever occurred to you that your distractions aren't distractions, but are actually the point (the context God is going to use to help you grow)? Explain.*

• The focus of the *Ascent* phase is moving your thoughts and feelings from introspection to prayer—presenting them to God.

• Be specific enough with your venting that you feel a weight off your chest for sharing, and brief enough that you don't get stuck in the mud.

• Don't pray earnestly about these things yet; that will come in the *Holy Place.*

• **Q:** *Why do you think it's so important to move our thoughts and feelings from introspection to prayer?*

• **Q:** *How do you think this discipline would affect your life long-term if you persisted in it?*

7

Entrance: Thanksgiving and Praise

The paradox of the previous chapter is this: You think your life is about you, but it's not. God knows that, and allows you to start there, with what's important to you—but he wants to help you get past yourself as soon as possible.

The Temple Pathway helps you do just that.

Hebrew worshippers ascending toward Jerusalem experienced what you'll also find, if you try biblical *Ascent*: a change in perspective. As we convert our introspective venting into prayer, a profound shift occurs: Our soul blinks, comes out of its stupor, stops looking at itself, and begins looking up to God. In this famous ascent song, the Psalm writer says, "I lift my eyes up to the hills—where does my help come from? My help comes from the Lord, the Maker of heaven and earth" (Psalm 121:1,2).

Oh yeah, I forgot.

One of the best ways to get over yourself is to cultivate a thankful, praise-filled heart toward God. By the time the venting Israelites arrived at the Temple gates, they had remembered the larger story unfolding in their lives and God's supreme place in it. Check this out:

> "Shout for joy to the Lord, all the earth. Worship the Lord with gladness; come before him with joyful songs. Know that the Lord is God. It is he who made us, and we are his; we are his people, the sheep of his pasture. *Enter his gates with thanksgiving and his courts with praise;* give thanks to him and praise his name. For the Lord is good and his love endures forever; his faithfulness continues through all generations" (Psalm 100, *emphasis mine*).

So yeah, do the *Ascent* thing. Vent and complain. Talk up your life with God. But at some point, as you reach the Temple gates, pause before you go further in. Ask God to help you make a thoughtful inventory of your life. What, specifically, are you thankful for?

Thanks-*giving*

It's not enough to feel grateful for what God has done. We need to give him thanks. The Father is looking for thanks-*giving,* not thanks-*feeling:*

> "On his way to Jerusalem, Jesus traveled along the border between Samaria and Galilee. As he was going into a village, ten men who had leprosy met him. They

stood at a distance and called out in a loud voice, "Jesus, Master, have pity on us!"

When he saw them, he said, "Go, show yourselves to the priests." And as they went, they were cleansed.

One of them, when he saw he was healed, came back, praising God in a loud voice. He threw himself at Jesus' feet and thanked him—and he was a Samaritan.

Jesus asked, "Were not all ten cleansed? Where are the other nine?" (Luke 17:11-17).

All ten lepers *felt grateful,* but only one took the time to express that gratitude in heartfelt thanks to Jesus. I want to be the one-in-ten!

Don't be religious about thanksgiving. Be real. Focus on the last twenty-four hours, and let the thanks flow. Once again, I recommend using simple bullet points to get the job done.

Thank God for answers to prayer, for special moments with friends and family. Thank him for cinnamon buns and warm jackets in fall. Thank him for the encouragement that found its way past your frustration, for laughter, for life, for the joy of your salvation. Thank him for difficult things too, trusting him to work all things for your good because you love him and are called according to his purpose. Thank him for strength, for what he's teaching you, and for how you're changing and growing in your faith. Thank him for his grace, his patience, his awesomeness. Thank him for the gospel, and that he's attentive to your every thought and emotion.

You know this. But did you know that how you *phrase* your thanksgiving is key? Consider these two offerings of thanksgiving to God:

"Father, thanks for dinner last night."

That's not bad. It gives God credit for the dinner by acknowledging it was a gift from him. But what if you gave God a more intentional gift of thanksgiving?

"Father, thank you for blessing our conversation and food around the table last night during dinner. It gave me such joy to connect with Bob and Bonnie again."

See? Not even close! And here's why: In the first example, you acknowledged God was involved in some unspecified way and deserved credit for how it turned out for some reason. But you weren't specific. It's kind of anemic, to be honest.

In the second example, by simply using a verb with an *ing*—*blessing*—you thanked God for the specific, active role he played in your evening. And by sharing some emotion connected to his involvement—joy—you told him why it meant so much to you. I'll get into why this is so important, but for now, here are some more examples:

"Thank you for awesome devotions yesterday" could become, "Thank you for *meeting* me in my devotions yesterday and *teaching* me so much about love. I *love* to learn and grow in you!"

"Thank you that I feel better this morning" could become, "Thank you for *answering* my prayer and *healing* my body. I feel *so much better*, and it's all because of you!"

"Thank you for my family," could become, "Thank you for *providing* such a loving family for me to grow up in. I'm so *blessed*."

My rule of thumb is to list a minimum of five things I'm thankful for each morning. Some days, it takes me awhile to list five things. Other days, my thank-you's could go on for a while. Sometimes they do! I write them down, but it's also powerful to speak our thanks out loud, to hear ourselves thanking God. Your soul needs regular reminders of God's ongoing goodness and care, and this will help.

Another tip: In your *thanksgiving*, try to include one 'future thank-you.' Let's say you're praying about a difficult meeting coming up. How do you think God wants to help you navigate that conversation? By giving you wisdom, maybe? And peace? Ask for that wisdom and peace, but then say thank you, by faith, ahead of time, for what he's going to do! I once heard someone say, "Thank-you is the language of trust." I love that. This is why Paul instructs us to offer our requests to God "with thanksgiving" (Philippians 4:6).

It could look like this in your prayers:

"Father, this meeting is a big one, as you well know. I'm worried about it and how it might play out. But thank you in advance that you will be with me. Thank you for the wisdom you will offer me throughout the conversation. I receive it now, ahead of time, by faith. And thank you for the peace you will flood me with as I look to you. In the name of Jesus, amen."

Powerful stuff!

Praising God

Do the *Ascent* thing. Vent to Jesus as you go. Then give him thanks for what he's done. Sit for a while and relish the good stuff with a grateful heart to God. Express your *thanksgiving* as clearly as possible. But then... please make sure you turn your *thanksgiving* into *praise*.

Thanksgiving is about expressing gratitude for *what God has done*; praise is expressing your admiration and approval for *who God is*. In this step, I review my *Ascent* and thanksgiving notes, and then ask, "What does this teach me about who God is?" Consider the examples I listed above. Those verbs I articulated in my thanksgiving come in handy: *blessing, meeting, teaching, answering, healing, and providing.*

Throughout the scriptures, there is a perfect harmony between God's works, his will, his ways, and his character. God always *works* in perfect harmony with his *ways*. His *ways* are always in alignment with his *will*. And his *will* is always a perfect expression of *who he is*.

Put another way, God does who he says he is. He provides because he is a Provider. He heals because he is is a Healer. He forgives because he is gracious. He loves because he is love. He delivers because he is a Deliverer. It's critically important that we make these connections because everything God does reveals his heart. The more clearly we see him, the more clearly we see everything else. The bigger our vision of God gets, the bigger and more robust our faith becomes.

When you're praising God, think in terms of two categories: traits and titles. It's great to tell God he's amazing, inspiring, incredible, and fantastic, but why is he amazing? Traits and titles flesh out what you mean by 'awesome.'

Traits are descriptions of his character—like holy, creative, kind, and loving. Let's go back to the verbs we listed. What do they tell us about who God is? Let's praise him for it.

We might say, "You're so generous, Lord! What an attentive Father. I love you!" Or, "I'm so humbled that Someone so great would stoop to take care of my needs!" Some days, you might see a thread of provision running through your list of thanksgiving. Other days, you might find yourself struck by his patience, moved by his pursuit of your heart, or humbled by his unending love. Praise him for those things.

Ascribing grand titles to God is also an important part of praising him. I think God loves it when we're creative with our praise titles, so long as they are accurate descriptions of his identity and character. Some of these are like 'nicknames' for God. For example, when God provided Abraham with a lamb for his sacrifice, Abraham came up with the title "Jehovah-Jireh"—The Lord provides (Genesis 22:12-14). That's the first time this name comes up in scripture, because Abraham created it on the spot.

The popular praise song "Way-Maker" by Nigerian gospel singer Sinach illustrates this so well: "Waymaker, miracle-worker, promise-keeper, light in the darkness; my God, that is who You are." Beautiful! How did she come up with these lyrics of praise? Perhaps God fulfilled a promise to her. Her thanksgiving became a title of praise, because this proves God is a promise-keeper. It's not just what he does; it's who he is.

When thanksgiving and praise don't come easy

What about when life is hard? What if you're stumbling through a dark valley full of confusion, loneliness, and pain? What if a grievous loss or a crippling wound cut you wide open? What if you find yourself deflated by discouragement or frustrated with failure? What if you don't feel particularly thankful? Here are a few thoughts to consider.

The Bible mandates offering thanksgiving to God. Further, many studies show that practicing gratitude is beneficial to our emotional and physical health—especially when life is painful. The Apostle Paul wrote, "Give thanks in all circumstances; for this is God's will for you in Christ Jesus" (I Thessalonians 5:18). Remember, God's will is "good, pleasing, and perfect" (Romans 12:2). He is worthy of all thanksgiving and praise, no matter how we feel about life.

We must learn to give thanks in all circumstances. The command carries a promise: If we're commanded to give thanks in every circumstance, then every circumstance must contain something to be thankful for! Paul isn't just sharing pretty words. Listen to what happened to him on one of his ministry journeys:

> "The crowd joined in the attack against Paul and Silas, and the magistrates ordered them to be stripped and beaten. After they had been severely flogged, they were thrown into prison, and the jailer was commanded to guard them carefully. Upon receiving such orders, he put them in the inner cell and fastened their feet in the

stocks. About midnight Paul and Silas were praying and singing hymns to God, and the other prisoners were listening to them. Suddenly there was such a violent earthquake that the foundations of the prison were shaken. At once all the prison doors flew open, and everybody's chains came loose." (Acts 16:22-26)

Incredible. Paul found himself chained to a wall for doing what God told him to do. He'd been beaten bloody, locked up because of his love for Jesus. And what does Paul do while wounds seep and bruises swell? He prays. He sings. He finds something to praise God for.

Was he insane? Nope. Look what happened next: God shook the foundations of the prison, the doors blew open, and his chains tumbled to the floor!

I'm not saying you haven't taken a beating. I'm not saying your abandonment isn't real, or that it doesn't hurt. I'm not saying life isn't dark, that you aren't in chains or that what happened to you is fair or right. I'm saying that turning your bitterness into praise will shake the foundation of the prison you're in.

I'm saying that defiantly thanking God for his goodness—even if it means thanking him that your left foot shackle isn't as tight as your right foot shackle—is going to open some prison doors. Especially the prison doors in your heart.

I'm saying looking to God with a grateful heart for his love and faithfulness is going to loosen those heavy chains of despair.

I'm saying that giving God thanks dispels darkness, begins the healing process, and clears the path for a new day. Your situation may not change, but your heart can be free as a bird within the prison you're in.

If you find that difficult, you're not alone. When our souls are heavy, thanksgiving comes hard. When that happens, it's time to sit down and talk to our soul—the part of us that doesn't want to lean into Jesus. David shows us how it's done. Note the verbs again (Forgives, heals, redeems, crowns, and satisfies):

> "Praise the Lord, O my soul; all my inmost being, praise his holy name. Praise the Lord, O my soul, and forget not all his benefits—who *forgives* all your sins, and *heals* all your diseases, who *redeems* your life from the pit and *crowns* you with love and compassion, who *satisfies* your desires with good things so that your life is renewed like the eagle's." (Psalm 103:1-5, *emphasis mine*).

The gospel is the power of God, so I think at least one of your *thanksgivings* each day should celebrate what Jesus has done for you and what it means for your current situation. Let's say you're feeling confused and stressed about your life at the moment, and your right shackle isn't any looser than your left shackle. There's nothing in your present that seems thank-worthy. What then?

It's time to review the good news of Jesus Christ, so you can use it to shore up your faith in the middle of the struggle:

Jesus lived the perfectly righteous life I could never live, then gave me the credit for his holiness. This frees me from the need to strive and prove myself as I rest in his justification instead of my performance.

Jesus loved me so much that he died in my place. He took the punishment I deserve for my sins, reconciling me with God so he could embrace me as his child. This frees me from the need to pay for my own failures or trying to please others to secure their love, earn their acceptance, or inflate my sense of worth.

Jesus rose from the dead and ascended to the right hand of God, defeating the power of sin, death, and the devil. He has seated me with him in the heavenly places, graced with his resurrection life and authority. This frees me from needing to produce personal victory and success in life.

Jesus poured out his Holy Spirit on me and indwells me. He has baptized me into his body, the Church. I am commissioned for service in his kingdom mission. He fills me with his power, purpose, character, and joy. I no longer need to pursue lesser things to fill and thrill me.

Jesus is preparing my eternal destiny in paradise, where he will fulfill every outstanding promise and shower me with unending delight. I will enjoy him face to face, forever. This frees me from needing to protect and preserve all the good things in my life, knowing that in Christ, the best is always yet to come.

My guess is that after standing under that waterfall of God's gospel goodness, you might forget what your struggle even was. But let's recap: You're feeling confused and stressed about your life at the moment. How can you turn the gospel into thanksgiving? Well, which element of the gospel applies most to your struggle? (You may need to review what I wrote in the last few paragraphs).

Let's try this out: "Father, I'm feeling stressed and confused right now. Jesus, thank you for living a perfect life so I don't have to. Thank you for giving me the credit for your perfect record. Thank you that you have already justified me, so no matter how this turns out, nothing can affect your loving verdict about me."

Or maybe: "Lord God, I'm feeling stressed and confused right now. But thank you for loving me so much that you died for me. Thank you for loving me no matter how well I perform (or not), because you died for me while I was still a sinner."

Powerful, right?

Thanksgiving and praise are critically important disciplines that build our faith in tangible ways. Thanksgiving trains us to apply the gospel to every area of life. It also teaches us to reflect on what's happening in our lives to discern God's active role in shaping our circumstances or answering our prayers. When you get in the thanksgiving habit, as I've described it in this chapter you'll start noticing God's fingerprints everywhere.

We praise God because he's worthy of our praises, but the benefits to us are profound. Praise trains us to see God's work as a natural overflow of his character, so that our sense of his power, glory, holiness, and worthiness expands in our thinking. The most exhilarating place to live is in the awe of God. This is partly what it means to "magnify the Lord" (Psalm 34:3, ESV).

Honestly, many mornings I already feel restored and inspired after my *Ascent*, *Thanksgiving*, and *Praise* practices. But we're not done yet. In fact, the Temple Pathway is just getting interesting!

Key points from this chapter:

• It's not enough to feel grateful for what God has done. We need to give him thanks.

• **Q**: *Do you agree that there is an important difference between being grateful and giving thanks? Explain.*

• Using an verb with an *'ing'* in our thanksgiving helps us think through God's active role in what we're thanking him for: *Thank you for **guiding** me.*

• **Q**: *Has your thanksgiving usually been vague and emotionless, or vivid and specific? Explain.*

• Thanksgiving is about expressing gratitude for *what God has done*; praise means expressing your admiration for *who God is*.

• No matter how painful life gets, we can thank and praise God for what Jesus has already done for us.

• The discipline of thankfulness builds our faith. It helps us apply the gospel, see God at work in our everyday lives, and grow in our awe of his goodness and love.

• **Q**: *Would you say that you regularly turn your gratitude into thanksgiving and praise? Why or why not?*

8

Heart-Check

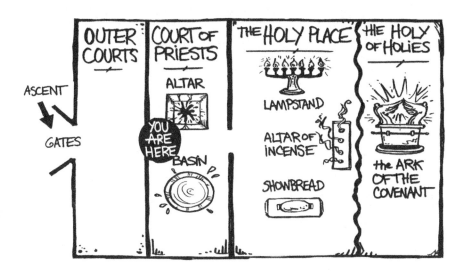

Open the eyes of your heart with me. Let's step into one of the most beautiful stories ever told. Engage your senses. Feel the tension. The Holy Spirit will guide you.

> "When one of the Pharisees invited Jesus to have dinner with him, he went to the Pharisee's house and reclined at the table. A woman in that town who lived a sinful life learned that Jesus was eating at the Pharisee's house, so she came there with an alabaster jar of perfume" (Luke 7:36,37).

It's already uncomfortable, isn't it? A Pharisee has invited Jesus for dinner, and a strange woman crashes the party. The moment she enters, both Jesus and the Pharisee know she's a sinful woman. That's because in

Jesus' day, prostitutes wore a vial of expensive perfume around their necks, strung onto a visible necklace. That vial, along with the distinctive aroma it carried, broadcasted that she was a prostitute for hire. Watch what happens next:

> "As she stood behind him at his feet weeping, she began to wet his feet with her tears. Then she wiped them with her hair, kissed them and poured perfume on them." (Luke 7:38)

Imagine the spike of panic this reputable Pharisee felt when 'prostitute perfume' began wafting out his windows! I have to chuckle as I picture him trying to explain the sensual aroma to the neighbours: "It's not what it smells like, honest!"

Let's focus on the woman, though. Consider how desperate for forgiveness she must be, risking even greater social condemnation for crashing a Pharisee's party. She's not trying to hide who she is or what she's done. If that were the case, she'd have ditched the perfume. She'd have changed into something more appropriate and covered her hair like good girls did.

When she arrives, she circles behind Jesus. Apparently, she's ashamed to face him. He's holy, and she's not, after all. She's crying—softly at first, but as she falls at Christ's bare feet, her sobbing intensifies. She's so emotional that she starts sprinkling his toes with her tears. Horrified at this indignity, she looks around for something to wipe away the mess she's making.

Finding nothing, she grabs a lock of her own hair and starts wiping. It's not working very well. This is when she sees it, dangling in front of her face between her and Jesus: *the vial of perfume.* That vial is the embodiment of her sinfulness, the emblem of her lostness. It's worth a full-year's wages—a pricey investment that helps her make money selling her body for sex at the cost of her soul.

At the sight of the vial, the woman's guilt and shame intensifies. She falters, wondering if she should salvage whatever dignity she has left and run from the house. But this is Jesus. She loves him, and she wants him to know it. She loves him so much, in fact, that she wants to leave her old life behind for good.

Watching that wretched vial swinging back and forth, she knows she doesn't want to vacillate in her faith like a pendulum. So she does the only thing she can think of doing; she uncorks the vial and dumps the entire aromatic mess on Jesus' feet. She hopes he understands what her bizarre gesture means—it's genuine confession, surrender, repentance, and love—all in one messy package. But it's coming from a prostitute, and at least one person in the room doesn't get it:

> "When the Pharisee who had invited him saw this, he said to himself, "If this man were a prophet, he would know who is touching him and what kind of woman she is—that she is a sinner." (Luke 7:39)

Jesus knows full well what kind of woman she is. And the woman knows what kind of woman she is. That much is clear. The real question is, does *the self-righteous Pharisee* know what kind of man *he* is? Does he grasp that he's just as much of a sinner as the woman? That he is equally in need of a Saviour? Do we? Do you? Do I?

> "Jesus answered him, "Simon, I have something to tell you."

Swap Simon's name for your own here. I'll do the same thing. Jesus has something to tell us.

> "Tell me, teacher," he said.

"Two people owed money to a certain moneylender. One owed him five hundred denarii, and the other fifty. Neither of them had the money to pay him back, so he forgave the debts of both. Now which of them will love him more?"

Simon replied, "I suppose the one who had the bigger debt forgiven."

"You have judged correctly," Jesus said. Then he turned toward the woman and said to Simon, "Do you see this woman? I came into your house. You did not give me any water for my feet, but she wet my feet with her tears and wiped them with her hair. You did not give me a kiss, but this woman, from the time I entered, has not stopped kissing my feet. You did not put oil on my head, but she has poured perfume on my feet. Therefore, I tell you, her many sins have been forgiven—as her great love has shown. But whoever has been forgiven little loves little." (Luke 7:40-47)

The prostitute understands how much forgiveness she needs. She knows she's hopelessly deep in the weeds. And she's already forgiven, by the way; the love she's pouring out on Jesus proves it. We could learn a thing or two from her. But the story isn't done yet.

"Then Jesus said to her, "Your sins are forgiven."

The other guests began to say among themselves, "Who is this who even forgives sins?"

Jesus said to the woman, "Your faith has saved you; go in peace." (Luke 7:48-50)

I want you to notice something: When Jesus spoke to Simon about the woman earlier, he said, "Her many sins *have been* forgiven." Past tense. And when Christ turns to the woman afterwards, he says, "Your sins are forgiven." Why did he repeat himself? Because he didn't just want to forgive her. He wanted her to *know* it. And he didn't just want her to *know* it, he wanted her to *feel* it: "Go in peace," Jesus said. A literal translation? "Go in untroubled, favoured, undisturbed well-being."

Simon's guests were confused by Jesus' expression of grace-on-the-spot. This kind of absolution was only supposed to happen in the Temple, accompanied by proper sacrifices, performed by official priests. But this is exactly what happened: Jesus, the ultimate High Priest, took her there himself.

Jesus can take us there, too, every single day. You and I can enter into his sacrifice to receive his grace anew. We can rise from our God-encounters filled with "untroubled, favoured, undisturbed well being."

How does that sound?

The Court of Priests, then and now

Throughout the Old Testament, the Court of Priests was the killing floor where a symbolic atonement was first *accomplished*, and then *applied*.

Atonement refers to a sacrifice for sin that releases God's forgiveness and reconciles us with him. To symbolize this atonement, Israel sacrificed innocent animals to the Lord. These animals shed their lifeblood on behalf of sinful, ritually-unclean people. But because these sacrifices were more symbol than substance—illustrating our need for grace until Christ had come—"the gifts and sacrifices being offered were not able to clear the conscience of the worshiper" (Hebrews 9:9). In fact, "those sacrifices (were) an annual *reminder* of sins" because "it is impossible for the blood of bulls and goats to take away sins" (Hebrews 10:3,4, *emphasis mine*).

Mind-boggling! After all the gruelling gore of Old Testament sacrifices, no one actually felt any better. Praise God, Jesus changed how we interact with the Court of Priests forever:

> "Christ did not enter a sanctuary made with human hands that was only a copy of the true one; he entered heaven itself, now to appear for us in God's presence. Nor did he enter heaven to offer himself again and again, the way the high priest enters the Most Holy Place every year with blood that is not his own. Otherwise Christ would have had to suffer many times since the creation of the world.
>
> But he has appeared once for all at the culmination of the ages to do away with sin by the sacrifice of himself. Just as people are destined to die once, and after that to face judgment, so Christ was sacrificed once to take away the sins of many" (Hebrews 9:24-28).

The sacrificial altar in the court of priests has been replaced by something infinitely more powerful—the cross of Christ. Jesus accomplished our atonement and reconciliation with God forever through his sacrificial death. We can rest in this gift forever, revelling in his finished work. Jesus has *achieved* our atonement. Our 'job' is to *apply* it.

The priests applied the atoning sacrificial blood by sprinkling it on everything. And by everything, I mean everything—from walls, to altars, to utensils, to priests, to the big toes on their right feet (Leviticus 14:14). This ritual illustrates our great and glorious task: to apply the shed blood of Christ by faith to everyone and everything in our lives:

> "Let us draw near to God with a sincere heart and with the full assurance that faith brings, having our hearts

sprinkled to cleanse us from a guilty conscience and having our bodies washed with pure water. Let us hold unswervingly to the hope we profess, for he who promised is faithful" (Hebrews 10:23,24).

What does this mean for us? The Court of Priests is no longer a place of sacrifice. It's where God wipes our guilt and shame away, where hearts are cleansed, where second chances flow from a never-ending fountain. Jesus didn't just *pay* our way to heaven. He *paved* the way for us to approach God directly and intimately, just like the sinful woman did. It's where we receive the grace of Christ's forgiveness. God's grace empowers us to repent for a changed life. No wonder Peter stated that "times of refreshing" would come from the Lord (Acts 3:19)!

Sacrifices performed in the Court of Priests occurred in broad daylight, on an altar situated just outside the 'Temple proper.' In the same way, the apostle John wrote, "If we walk in the light, as he is in the light, we have fellowship with one another, and the blood of Jesus, his Son, purifies us from all sin" (I John 1:7). We're meant to walk in the light but we regularly stray, drifting into shadow and darkness. God calls us back into his searching light in the Court of Priests every day, starting with what I like to call a 'Heart-Check.'

My Heart-Check starts with a personal review. I often pray a prayer like David prayed in Psalm 139:23,24: "Search me, God, and know my heart; test me and know my anxious thoughts. See if there is any offensive way in me, and lead me in the way everlasting."

This simple prayer invites God to shine the light of his truth on my soul. I want him to remind me of things I thought, said, and did that are sinful and put me "out of step" with the Holy Spirit. This is not introspection. I rely on the Holy Spirit's convicting presence to show me what I need to see—nothing more, and nothing less.

Next, I meander through yesterday's memories, opening them to the Holy Spirit's conviction and direction. I've found it powerful to bring my 'brain-dump' from the *Ascent* stage into the light at this point. The Holy Spirit will highlight two kinds of truths: what *grieved his heart,* and what *quenched his work.*

Grieving God's heart

We grieve God's heart by thinking, choosing, and doing things we *shouldn't* do (Psalm 78:40, Ezekiel 6:9). This includes outright disobedience and un-Christlike behaviours like lying, cheating, or hurting others. We can also grieve the Holy Spirit by embracing ungodly motives and entertaining unhealthy attitudes. This includes internal vices—indulging our pride, selfishness, lust, or anger.

Even 'small' sins can trigger massive avalanches in our lives. I'd like to think Adam and Eve were shocked by the repercussions of eating a single forbidden fruit. Paul reminds us that "sin entered the world through one man, and death through sin, and in this way death came to all people, because all sinned" (Romans 5:12). All of creation is now in "bondage to decay" (Romans 8:21) and "has been groaning as in the pains of childbirth" as it awaits God's promised redemption (Romans 8:22).

Acting out sin incarnates the kingdom of darkness and gives the devil a foothold in the real world (Ephesians 4:25-31). Jesus wants to set us free from all bondage to sin, death, and the devil so we can manifest his kingdom instead.

Quenching God's work

If we grieve the Holy Spirit's heart by thinking, choosing, and doing things we *shouldn't* do, we quench the Holy Spirit's work by *not* doing things he *wants* us to do. Quenching the Spirit means not letting God express himself through us (I Thess. 5:16-20). This includes sins of omission: "If anyone, then, knows the good they ought to do and doesn't do it, it is sin for them" (James 4:17).

Did you shrink back from taking a risk or stepping out in faith? Were you supposed to say something, but held your tongue instead? Did you sense a prompting from the Holy Spirit to love someone tangibly, but ignored God's leading instead of obeying it? This quenches the flow of the Spirit. While grieving the Spirit manifests the kingdom of darkness, quenching the Spirit prevents the kingdom of God from manifesting in the world.

A few words about our sin

One of the classic verses people quote about sin is Isaiah 59:2: "Your iniquities have separated you from your God; your sins have hidden his face from you, so that he will not hear." God spoke those words to the nation of Israel before Jesus paid the ultimate price for our atonement. Our sins *used to* separate us from God, but after putting our faith in Jesus, nothing can separate us from God and his love (Romans 8:38,39).

God doesn't want us to confess our sins because they separate us from him. He wants us to confess our sins because they're hurting us and others. God doesn't hide his face from us, but sin obscures our view of his grace and glory. Confession restores our spiritual eyesight. As God cleanses us from all unrighteousness, the active flow of his grace is restored in and through us.

It's not our job to dredge the bottom of our souls looking for sin to confess. That would be endless, fruitless, and lead us into despair. Instead, we simply come into God's light and let him reveal what we need to see. Jesus promised the Holy Spirit would guide us into all truth (John 16:13). We need to trust him to do just that.

Some Christians reject the idea that God convicts his children of sin once they've received Jesus. He most certainly does! In his letters to the churches in Revelation, Jesus says repeatedly, "I hold this against you" (Revelation 2:4,14,20). He then names specific sins he expects them to deal with. God is saying, "There's something you're doing (or not doing) that's hurting you and hurting others. I love you too much to let it go, so let's deal with it."

Jesus loves us in the same way. He highlights something, then we confess what God has highlighted. We can trust him to reveal what we need to address in order to restore full harmony with his Holy Spirit. This doesn't mean we've perfectly confessed every micro-sin within us. It means we've addressed what he highlighted. He expects nothing more, and nothing less.

If that seems too vague, maybe magnets will help. Did you ever play with magnets as a kid? A magnet's power is caused by a high degree of atomic alignment (A). This alignment creates a magnetic field, which then has the power to attract materials that contain iron (B).

Once an object has been 'grabbed' by the magnet's field, the magnet goes to work on it, re-aligning what is misaligned within it. Over time, the magnet will transform the chaotic internal domains of the new object, pulling it into greater alignment with itself.

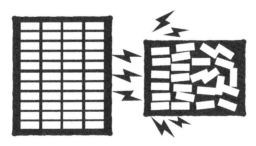

This is part of what it means to be transformed into Christ's image.

God is infinitely holy, loving, and pure. He exists in a state of perfect alignment and integrity within himself. You and I, on the other hand, are a chaotic mess, corrupted by sin. Our internal integrity is painfully out of alignment with God's character, will, and ways. Every idea, value, desire, decision, behaviour, thought, philosophy and motive we hold that is not aligned with God is a problem. This doesn't separate us from his love, but it puts us at odds with his purposes and the life he created us to live. It grieves and quenches God's Spirit.

God invites us to lay our lives down on his altar every day. As we still our minds and meet with the Father, he draws us to himself so he can exert his magnetic influence on us. United with him, we meditate on his word and he transforms us into his glorious image. Truth by truth, lie by lie, value by value, we are gradually realigned with his heart. He won't stop realigning us until we become magnetic too, resonating with his heart and holiness. We don't change by trying to change; we change by giving ourselves more fully to God.

I kick-start each morning with this realignment process as God guides me through the Temple Pathway. Along the way, I give him my 'big four'—my attention, affection, dependence, and obedience. As the Father lays fresh claim to me, the Holy Spirit addresses things within me that are not like Jesus. When I see these issues, I confess them and repent to align with God in that area of my life. I can't imagine following Jesus without this transforming interaction with him.

I've been opening myself to the Spirit's conviction almost every day for over thirty years. Along the way, I've noticed something profound: he certainly brings up single sins, like snapping at my kids or shrinking back from doing the right thing in the heat of a moment. But if you make confession a habit, you'll also realize how unoriginal you are. You'll notice the same issues come up over and over.

These aren't just 'one-off' sins, but the broken *ways* we typically handle life. That's why David asked God to show him the "offensive *ways*" in him that led him away from God's "*way* everlasting" (Psalm 139:23,24). It's also why John called us to "*walk* in the light" (I John 1:7).

Most sin we confess isn't just something we *did*; it's something we *do*. God is most concerned with the things we do—or avoid—again and again. When we do sinful things repeatedly, they become our ways. Think of ways as habitual pathways.

When the seed of God's truth 'lands' on our habitual pathways, they rarely germinate. Why? Because habits run on autopilot, not mental energy. When God sends his truth to address or correct our habits, we're too busy motoring along in our normal ways to receive or even perceive it. The enemy snatches away the seed God is trying to plant, and we remain stuck in our sin (Matthew 13:19).

You have a *way* of doing just about everything: The way you handle stress; the way you deal with (or avoid!) conflict, or the way you approach tough conversations. There is a way you wind down for the day, a way of reading the Bible, a way you approach the future, politics, or church. There's even a way you drive to work every morning!

When sinful attitudes shape our ways, they lead us into unhealthy places and thwart our purpose in Christ. When our ways are transformed by God, we begin walking in God's ways. This is the path of life, where we can embrace our true destiny for God's glory.

When you make Heart-Checks a daily discipline, the patterns created by your ongoing confessions will reveal your sinful ways, so God can address and correct them. If you find yourself repeating the same sins, I highly recommend that you read my crash course in Repentance in the final section of this book.

Key points from this chapter:

• Our forgiveness has been accomplished through Christ's blood shed for us. Now we need to apply his blood to everything that needs his grace.

• God wants us to come into his searching light for regular heart checks.

• God will convict us of individual sins, but he is more concerned with illuminating our sinful ways so he can lead us in his everlasting ways.

• Our sins fall into two categories: Grieving the Spirit by *doing* things we *shouldn't*, and quenching the Spirit by *not* doing things we *should*.

• When we grieve the Holy Spirit by doing and saying things we shouldn't, we manifest the kingdom of darkness around us.

• When we quench the Holy Spirit's work, we prevent the kingdom of God from manifesting in the world.

• God exerts his magnetic influence over us as we spend time with him, gradually bringing us into alignment with his heart and character.

• Q: *How has this chapter expanded or changed your view of sin and how it affects your relationship with God?*

• Q: *Most people think of confession as focusing on individual sins. What did you learn about learning to discern and confess your sinful ways?*

• Q: *What are some of your common 'ways' of both grieving and quenching the Spirit?*

9

Confession and Grace

So far, we've learned that the Court of Priests begins with coming into God's light for a Heart-Check. The Holy Spirit will reveal two kinds of sin: how we've grieved his heart and how we've quenched his work.

Our next step in the Court of Priests is confession. When the Holy Spirit shows us something, our job is simply to agree with his assessment. That's what confession is—agreement. He says, "Brad, that's sin." I say, "I agree. You're absolutely right. I've sinned."

By the way, we're all experts at spiritual agreement. It's just that we've been agreeing with the lies of the enemy! This is important to realize, because agreements form partnerships. I want to partner with Jesus, not the devil. The first step is agreeing with Jesus, because Jesus is always right.

During your confession, don't make excuses. Don't rationalize. Let God convict you. You're guilty as charged. The more we agree with God, the more like Jesus we become. The more we resonate with Jesus, the better we're positioned to partner with him in the world.

Also remember: We're not confessing our sins to fix our relationship with God. Jesus bore that responsibility for us. His work is forever perfect, complete, and effective. If confession could fix what sin broke, then Christ's work was not enough and reconciliation with God would be up to us. This is a gross misunderstanding of the gospel.

If our sins are already paid for and forgiven, why does God want us to confess them? There are several reasons:

- He wants us to take responsibility for our failures
- He wants us to remember the price Jesus paid for us
- We need to address how our sin is hurting us and others
- He wants to transform us into Christ's image over time

Giving and receiving grace

Remember the sinful woman we followed to the feet of Jesus? Christ said she'd already been forgiven, but that wasn't enough. He wanted her to know and feel forgiven. And that's what he wants for us, too. We're not fully free until we *feel* forgiven. From God's perspective, we're already forgiven, but we're still bound by our painful emotions as though we're still guilty. After our Heart-Check, we Confess our sin— but the final step in the Court of Priests pausing to Give and Receive Grace.

To *forgive* means to release or cancel a debt. Christ has already cancelled our debt at the cross. God has already released us from the judgment we deserve. This is what God wants us to believe, so we can live free, "in view of God's mercy" (Romans 12:1).

The second and equally important sense of the word *forgive* is "to lift up and carry away." This is often what's missing in our experience of both giving and receiving forgiveness. God has released us from our debt, but we're still bound by our guilt and shame. Or we've said, "I forgive Susan," but still feel anger or bitterness towards her. In both cases, God wants us to feel the power of his cleansing, so that we can "go in peace." Once again, we're not fully free until we feel it.

How does God set us free from these natural, negative emotions? He lifts them off of our souls and carries them away. If we're confessing our own sin, he lifts our guilt and shame away, separating us from their power forever. If we're forgiving another person, he lifts our hate, anger, and bitterness away, excising them from our souls like venom from a snakebite.

Forgiveness is a relational transaction—a tangible release of guilt, shame, and anger. When we forgive, we participate in a real, live gospel-exchange with God. Christ actively absorbs our guilt, shame, anger, and bitterness, then replaces them with his grace and peace. This isn't merely a theological concept, occurring somewhere in the ledgers of heaven; it's something God actually does in our hearts and minds. I've watched him do it a thousand times.

When I confess my sin (or when I forgive others), I picture this lifting and releasing actually happening—because it is. I thank God by faith for his grace and forgiveness, and imagine myself free from guilt and shame. I thank God that I'm pure because his blood has released me from my sin. Sometimes I picture being washed by a beautiful waterfall of grace, or envision Christ lifting the burden from my shoulders. I always praise him for his perfect cleansing work.

And just like the sinful woman, I *feel* forgiven. Jesus would never die on the cross for my sin and leave me a miserable wretch to "go in heaviness, regret, and shame" instead of filling me with peace. Not in a million years!

He also wants me to be free from anger and bitterness so that I stop infecting my relationships with their poison. I may be justifiably angry about how someone treated me, but hanging onto anger only hurts me and people close to me. Forgiving releases God's healing and empowering grace into my heart. It also releases that same grace into the situation that frustrates me.

When I'm forgiving others (or helping others forgive those who have hurt them), I walk through a simple process in prayer with God:

1.   I verbally unpack what the person did to me, in detail.

2.   I express how this injustice made me feel—expressing that fully, as best I can.

3.   I admit how that makes me feel towards them now (anger, bitterness, rage, frustration, etc). The key here is allowing our buried emotions to rise up and take centre-stage in God's light. Don't worry, they won't have the limelight for long. * *Please note: Confess how you actually feel, not how you think you ought to feel or wish you felt.*

When this is done I pray (or have the person I'm guiding pray) something like this:

> "Father, I release (name) to your justice and grace, for (what they did to me) and for making me feel (how their offence hurt me)."

> "I also release (listing all my negative emotions towards them) to you, Jesus. I don't want to carry this anymore. Come lift all of this (list the emotions again) from my soul right now, and replace it with your grace and peace. Amen."

Trust me, God's healing work will blow your mind.

I once read a Facebook post that missed the gospel so badly, it made my heart ache. It read, "The closer you get to God, the more sinful you will feel." That's an Old Testament sentiment! In the new and living way of Christ, the closer I get to him, the more *forgiven* I feel. The more gratitude I feel. The more praise I express. My sin is serious, but I don't feel more sinful, I feel more thankful.

If you still feel guilty for something, it's because your interaction with Christ is not complete. Either you haven't fully confessed or owned your sin, or you haven't fully given him your guilt and shame. Don't move on until you've experienced the life-changing forgiveness of Jesus Christ. Linger until your heart is free and you know it, so you can "go in peace."

Pleasing God

I have wonderful news for you: God doesn't just want to reveal and address what you're getting *wrong*. He's also eager to highlight and celebrate what you're getting *right*. He wants you to know what pleased him so he can affirm you for it. Receiving God's grace includes receiving his affirmation.

Let's return to the sinful woman—the prostitute—who threw herself at the feet of Jesus. She was right to repent. Her sin was a big deal! But please don't miss what Jesus said about her. Can you imagine what she felt in her soul as he spoke these gracious words?

> "Do you see this woman? I came into your house. You did not give me any water for my feet, but she wet my feet with her tears and wiped them with her hair. You did not give me a kiss, but this woman, from the time I entered, has not stopped kissing my feet. You did not put oil on my head, but she has poured perfume on my feet" (Luke 7:44,45).

God is perfectly holy, but he sent Jesus to deal with our sin problem forever. He now sees us through the perfect righteousness of Christ. This means God isn't perpetually disappointed in you. He's not expecting you to get things right all the time. In fact, as a good Father, he's eager to affirm you for your growth and progress—even when you're failing regularly along the way.

God wants us to "make it our goal to please him" (II Corinthians 5:9) and to "live a life worthy of the Lord and please him in every way" (Colossians 1:10). But how can we know if we're succeeding in that mission? How can I know which of my ways please him? Certainly the Bible helps frame the target, but is that all there is to it? Just studying the Bible and measuring ourselves against it?

In the Court of Priests, we've come into the light to have our soul and actions audited by God. We've confessed our sin and received his grace and forgiveness. But Jesus also said, "Whoever lives by the truth comes into the light, so that it may be seen plainly that what they have done has been done in the sight of God" (John 3:21). His light doesn't just expose our sin. It also illuminates our faithfulness. Two chapters later, Jesus poses an important question:

> "How is it possible for you to believe [how can you learn
> to believe], you who [are content to seek and] receive
> praise *and* honor *and* glory from one another, and yet
> do not seek the praise *and* honor *and* glory which come
> from Him Who alone is God?" (John 5:44, Amplified
> Bible, Classic Edition)

Our faith can't grow to its full stature without hearing from God about what pleases him. Receiving God's "well done" isn't something the Father reserves for heaven. He wants us to receive it here and now, on a daily basis. In fact, Jesus tells us to *seek it out*. I believe receiving affirmation from God might just be one of the most important disciplines we can master.

When I preach a sermon, I pour out everything I have. I try to put my best thinking and creative prowess into my preparation so I can speak from the heart. Even so, after I've delivered each message, a whisper of doubt creeps in: *Was that any good? How did I do? Was it clear? Did people get it? Will it even make a difference?*

"Seek praise, honour, and affirmation from the only One who matters," Jesus says. Why? Because he wants to affirm what's worth affirming, and we desperately need it from him. If I don't draw my affirmation from the Father, I'll go looking for it somewhere else. There is no other voice I can fully trust to give me the truth, the whole truth, and nothing but the truth.

After preaching, I often just look to the Father and ask, "How'd I do, Dad?" And then listen for his response. Sometimes he shares a critique or two. Most often I hear something like, "You did well, Son. Thank you."

Please note: this doesn't mean my delivery was perfect. It doesn't mean that my motives were absolutely pure, or that my faith and love were one-hundred percent on the mark. It means there was something in me that pleased God, something he thought was worth celebrating.

When Jesus wrote letters to his churches in Revelation chapters 2 and 3, he includes helpful critiques like I described above. This seems natural to us. But he spends just as much time affirming the believers for what they're getting right as he does addressing what they've gotten wrong. Christ begins all but one of these letters affirming something the believers are doing well. Two of the churches, Smyrna and Philadelphia, only receive affirmations from Christ; Laodicea only receives a critique.

This is Jesus, remember—the One who never changes. In these letters, Christ is doing what he always does—so we can anticipate him doing the same thing for us.

Here's what I recommend: while you're walking in the light in the Court of Priests, ask God a simple question. You could phrase it something like this: *Father, is there anything you would like to affirm in me today? Is there anything I've done or said that pleased you or made you smile?*

Trust me, you'll be pleasantly surprised at what you hear. After posing the question, sit in it for a minute or two. Allow him to remind you of key moments from your day—kind words you spoke, perhaps how you resisted a temptation, bit your tongue, or put your own needs aside to serve someone else. If he reveals something to you (if things come to mind), thank him for his affirmation. Take a deep breath, and sit in it for a moment.

You can follow up with a second question: *Why did that please you, Father? Why was that important to you? I'd really like to know.*

This honours Paul's admonition to "find out what pleases the Lord" (Ephesians 5:10). It also empowers us to do more of what he loves. Living to make God smile sounds like an amazing way to live.

You may have a few 'Laodicea days' when God doesn't affirm you for much, or anything at all. But you also may have a few 'Philly' days, when he only has good things to point out. Remember, this isn't because you've been perfect; it just means there is nothing big he wants to address that day. Relish the blessing.

To recap, our Heart-Check in the Court of Priests is about coming into God's searching light. He will reveal what grieves his heart, what quenches his work, and what pleases him. In the next two chapters, we'll explore what to do with what he shows us.

Key points from this chapter:

- Confession is simply agreeing with God about our sin.

- God want us to confess our sins for several reasons:
    - He wants us to take responsibility for our failures
    - He wants us to remember the price Jesus paid for us
    - We need to address how our sin is hurting us and others
    - He wants to transform us into Christ's image over time

- Forgiveness is about canceling our debt, but it's also about lifting away our guilt and shame so we can "go in peace."

- Forgiveness is a relational transaction—a tangible release of guilt, shame, and anger in exchange for his grace and peace.

- **Q:** *How has this chapter expanded or challenged your concept of confession and forgiveness?*

- In the new and living way of Christ, the closer I get to him, the more *forgiven* I feel.

- I'm not totally free until I *feel* forgiven—until I'm released from the guilt and shame I hold against myself.

- **Q:** *Have you ever experienced God's forgiveness as a tangible release from guilt and shame? Explain.*

- God also wants to illuminate what we're getting right so we can receive his affirmation and learn to please him more.

- **Q:** *What do you think of creating a regular discipline around seeking God's affirmation for what you're getting right? Has this been part of your spiritual practices before? Why or why not?*

10

Revelation and Prayer

So far, you've vented the concerns of your heart to God in your *Ascent*. You've focused your mind on him through *Thanksgiving* and *Praise*. You've come into God's light for a *Heart-Check*, then *confessed* your sin. You have both *given and received God's unfathomable grace*. And finally, you have received his *affirmation*, reflecting on what pleases him.

So good, right? But there are three more spiritual practices to learn. Next stop: the Holy Place. This is a sacred space of *Revelation* and *Spirit-led prayer.*

If you could step into the ancient Holy Place, you would notice three stunning pieces of furniture. To your right, a table featuring loaves of bread; to your left, a tall, solid-gold lampstand; and directly ahead, a beautiful altar for burning incense.

Each piece is a powerful symbol that represents an important spiritual practice. Each of these practices opens up a life-changing experience with God. Let's unpack them and revel in what they represent for us.

The Bread of the Presence: Wisdom from Christ and his word

The table to your right displays twelve fresh loaves of bread (Exodus 25:23-30). This bread (usually covered) was called both "showbread" (Numbers 4:7) and "the bread of the presence" (Exodus 25:30) throughout the Old Testament. Faithful priests replaced the loaves once a week with fresh bread, after which they could eat the older ones.

Bread is a powerful symbol throughout the scriptures. When the Hebrews marched out of their bondage in Egypt, they "ate the manna in the wilderness; as it is written, 'He gave them bread from heaven to eat" (John 6:31). Millenia later, Jesus stated, "I am the bread of life," and "the one who feeds on me will live because of me" (John 6:35,57).

Jesus is the spiritual manna that sustains you throughout your life. Your spirit needs Christ like your body needs food! Because Jesus is also the Word of God made flesh (John 1:14), the showbread symbolizes the spiritual sustenance and substance we receive through communion with Christ and digesting the scriptures.

The loaves were called the *bread of the presence* because whey were visual proof that God had been present—tangibly enough to provide the wheat to bake it. They were called *showbread* because they demonstrated God's faithfulness and care. Yesterday's provision says, "Look, taste, and see! God has been faithful! You have never been alone."

This declaration also stands as a prophetic promise of the Father's faithfulness in the future. Jesus instructed us to pray for "our daily bread," anticipating God's generous response. He's eager to meet our physical needs, drawing endless blessings from his riches in glory to sustain us (Philippians 4:19). Here we draw from the thanksgiving and praises we offered him at the Temple gates. Our hope finds nourishment as we relish his attentive care.

God's faithfulness is proclaimed through the scriptures and proven through his provision and promise-keeping. He graciously allows us to partake of his presence, strength, joy, power, companionship, guidance, mercy, and illumination. He promises to provide all our genuine needs —physical, spiritual, emotional, mental, social, and everything in between. Best of all, he provided Jesus. Christ is our sacrificial lamb who takes away the sins of the world. God has provided, he is providing, and he will provide, because he is an ever-present Provider. His goodness and faithfulness are the foundations of the cosmos.

Finally, the twelve loaves symbolize all twelve tribes of Israel—the entire family of God. His presence and provision is more than enough for all of us!

God will speak to you throughout this Temple Pathway, but the Holy Place is like a listening chamber. The bread of the presence reminds us to meditate on the Bible, his written word. As you study your Bible, Jesus will teach you, correct you, offer direction, share important insights about your life, and reveal more of who he is. * *Please take the time to dive into my short crash course in Bible Study in the next section of this book.*

As we meditate on God's word and consider his faithfulness, we recall and speak out God's promises (Psalm 119:148). As Paul the Apostle wrote, "No matter how many promises God has made, they are "Yes" in Christ. And so through him the "Amen" is spoken by us to the glory of God" (II Corinthians 1:20). The more we agree with God, the more his kingdom comes in us. This begins with God's written word in the scriptures, but also includes words or promises God has spoken to us personally—things we've recorded in previous journal entries.

There is nothing 'magic' or 'name it and claim it' about this. We simply honour God by offering our 'amen' to his promises. We declare our faith in God by believing what he's already said. As we rehearse his promises, we experience his ongoing faithfulness. Agreement with God activates a partnership with him in that truth. As I've already referenced, "It is written: I believed; therefore I have spoken." Since we have that same spirit of faith, we also believe and therefore speak" (II Corinthians 4:13).

The North American church seems preoccupied with getting a 'new word' from God. This is certainly common in more charismatic traditions, but it's found in conservative circles as well. We're encouraged to read (and learn!) something new in the Bible every day. Each weekend, we receive a new word from the scriptures that we're expected to digest and live out. Pastors try not to repeat themselves or revisit common themes because they feel the pressure to 'preach the whole counsel of God.'

This is problematic. As the Apostle James writes, "Do not merely listen to the word, and so deceive yourselves. Do what it says" (James 1:22). I believe our steady diet of 'new' teachings is actually training us to deceive ourselves. We never marinate in God's word, pausing in a passage until we truly 'get it,' or better yet, until it *gets us*. I would rather soak in one scripture until it transforms me than accumulate knowledge that deceives me into thinking I'm growing in my faith. The 'new word' mentality can fool us into believing that accumulating information equals spiritual growth. That's a lie. Spiritual growth only occurs when we put the word into practice.

Friends, meditate on what God has already said. Chew on his promises to you. Review what you studied last week. Circle around to evaluate whether it's changed you. Be honest about whether you've done anything with it. Be willing to park there until the word has accomplished what God desires and has achieved the purpose for which he sent it (Isaiah 55:11).

When the challenges we're facing stir up doubts in us, the Holy Place teaches us to employ what I call "faith-logic." Faith-logic looks back at what God has done, understanding that nearly everything God did is something God still does—because God does who he says he is. But faith-logic doesn't stop there. It pulls our past experience with God into the current situation, and even into our future. When David faced off with the Philistine juggernaut, Goliath, he said,

> "Your servant has killed both the lion and the bear; this uncircumcised Philistine will be like one of them, because he has defied the armies of the living God. The Lord who rescued me from the paw of the lion and the paw of the bear will rescue me from the hand of this Philistine" (II Samuel 17:36,37).

That's faith-logic in action. Abraham modelled it for us, too:

> "By faith Abraham, when God tested him, offered Isaac as a sacrifice. He who had embraced the promises was about to sacrifice his one and only son, even though God had said to him, "It is through Isaac that your offspring will be reckoned." Abraham reasoned that God could even raise the dead, and so in a manner of speaking he did receive Isaac back from death" (Hebrews 11:17-19).

As God renews our minds, our faith-logic improves. God's word really is a feast. As we speak it out and live by faith in what he says, that feast takes shape in the world around us. We must meditate on what God has spoken, letting his word reform our reason and fill our mouths with truth. This grounds us in God's reality instead of being sucked into what the world is saying.

The Lampstand: Wisdom from the Holy Spirit

Opposite the bread of the presence sits a stunning lampstand hammered from pure gold. Seven branches fan out from the base, curving upwards into golden almond buds and blossoms. In each of the seven blossoms, candle flames are flickering. Twice a day, the priests trim the wicks and replenish the olive oil feeding them. Their flames are meant to burn continuously (Exodus 27:20,21).

Once again, the symbolism is rich and multilayered. While the bread symbolizes the work of Jesus, the oil-powered lampstand symbolizes the flow of the Holy Spirit.

The structure of the lampstand mirrors a beautiful almond tree. There is a central shaft, flanked by three branches on each side—seven channels in total. The central shaft represents God, while the remaining six represent every aspect of human life (*six* is the biblical number for humanity; *seven* represents covenant and completion).

Visually, oil flows into each of these channels, providing the fuel for each wick. Throughout scripture, light is symbolic of the presence of God and his revelation of truth (Psalm 43:3). The lampstand reminds us that the Holy Spirit wants to flow into every area of our lives. He longs to release divine wisdom into whatever we do.

The cups, crafted into almond buds and blossoms, foretell the fruit we can expect when the Holy Spirit's wisdom is flowing. Apparently, almond trees are the first trees to awaken after winter each year in Israel and their buds emerge just before the Spring arrives. The lampstand helps us take hold of God's fruit by faith—even before it arrives! This is how Abraham could make himself at home in the promised land before he fully inherited it.

The lampstand reminds us to listen to the constant wisdom flowing from the Holy Spirit. I hear God's voice most clearly in the Holy Place. The Temple Pathway purifies my thinking and sharpens my discernment. As we listen here, God gives us clearer hindsight (his perspective on what's happened to us); clearer insight (his perspective on what's happening to us); and clearer foresight (information we need to face what's going to happen in our lives).

It's truly mind-boggling how many inspiring, practical, helpful, and Christ-centred ideas 'occur to me' in the Holy Place. That's not because I'm smart or spiritual. The 'Temple Pathway' has done its work, opening my spiritual eyes and ears to what God wants to reveal. I'm not actually discovering anything; truth is being revealed to me. The Holy Place is a place of revelation.

As I move through the Temple Pathway, something beautiful takes place: What's on God's heart eclipses what is on mine. The urgency of what I've been thinking dissolves into a desire to know what the Father is thinking. Jesus is a constant and loyal Friend to us, but he's looking for people willing to return the favour. How do you know if you've become a friend to God? He lets you in on his plans. He confides in you. He shares his heart with you (James 2:23; Genesis 18:18,19; John 15:15).

During this time of listening and conversation, circle back around to the issues you recorded in the *Ascent* phase. Ask the Holy Spirit to guide you into all truth about each one. Ask him what you've been missing— what's on his heart for you, what he'd like you to know about each situation. Ask him what he'd like you to do about what he reveals. Write down what he says. God will surprise you with guidance and insight you couldn't have come up with on your own.

The Altar of Incense: Spirit-led prayer

The altar of incense is a place of prayer directed to the Father. By the way, this is the spot where Zechariah was standing in the Temple when the angel Gabriel appeared to him:

> "While he was serving as priest before God when his division was on duty, according to the custom of the

priesthood, he was chosen by lot to enter the temple of the Lord and burn incense.

And the whole multitude of the people were praying outside at the hour of incense. And there appeared to him an angel of the Lord standing on the right side of the altar of incense. And Zechariah was troubled when he saw him, and fear fell upon him.

But the angel said to him, "Do not be afraid, Zechariah, for your prayer has been heard, and your wife Elizabeth will bear you a son, and you shall call his name John" (Luke 1:8-13).

Awesome. And when John the Apostle got a day trip to heaven through an amazing vision, he was shown the *heavenly* version of the altar of incense:

"Then I saw a Lamb, looking like it had been slain, standing in the centre of the throne, encircled by the four living creatures... each one had a harp and they were holding golden bowls full of incense, which are the prayers of the saints" (Revelation 5:6,8).

Now it's time to *pray*.

"Wait a minute," I can hear you saying. "I've already been praying, starting with my *Ascent* stuff. Didn't that count?"

I guess you could call that praying. But it was more like venting. God met you where you were. Since then, you've thanked and praised him. You've received forgiveness and have forgiven others. You've repented of your sin. You've listened to God and meditated on his word. And now you're standing to pray, infused with a sense of Christ's presence and promise for ongoing provision—inspired by the fruit-producing revelation of the Holy Spirit!

You may have *prayed* earlier, but not like *that*. Believe me, you'll sense the difference.

And there's more. These prayers are offered at an altar, a place of surrender. This is why Jesus taught us to pray, "Our father in heaven, holy be your name. Your kingdom come, your will be done, on earth as it is in heaven" (Matthew 6:9,10). True prayer is about us submitting to the rule of God in our lives. It's about making Jesus' desires and dreams come true. As we submit to his will, we learn to long for the same things he's longing for.

So yes, lay your requests before God. But in the Holy Place, you're praying from the posture God has been wanting from you all along: Spirit-led dependence. This is where mountains move, where God unleashes miracles, where the word of God becomes the will of God in your life. Praying from this posture becomes more of a conversation with God than the grocery list you offered him on the way up the hill. So don't rush things.

I also need to point out that while the priests certainly prayed for themselves and their own concerns, their primary role was to intercede for God's people. Jesus taught us to pray for "*our* daily bread" and "those who trespass against *us*" (Matthew 6:11,12). So pray for your *us*. Pray for family, friends, and people in your inner circle.

But that's not all. Believers in Jesus also function as a kingdom of priests to the rest of the world (Revelation 1:6). A huge part of our purpose is to pray for the lost and live to help them connect with God, just like Old Testament priests did for the Israelites. The broken world breaks God's heart. As we pray, we join him in his mission to rescue the lost through King Jesus.

Now is the time to revisit the things you vented during your *Ascent*. You'll see those issues differently now. In this place of revelation, take time to listen to God address what you shared earlier. Ask him, "What would you like me to know about this?" Listen for his word, then use these insights from God in your prayers.

For example, you might have vented about your idiot coworker during *Ascent*: "Bob makes me so mad. He totally threw me under the bus again during staff meeting!" But then you took a few minutes to thank and praise God for his goodness to you. You softened a little, didn't you?

Next, you came to the cross and realized your response to Bob was over-the-top. You confessed that and received God's grace. You also forgave Bob for his outburst, and let the grace of God wash over you once again.

Now, in the Holy Place, you can come back to the conflict and ask for God's perspective on what happened. His perspective is far different than yours. Now you pray for the relationship to be restored. You ask for a better attitude and patience to deal with Bob next time. Perhaps you sense God's deep love for him and pray he would one day respond to Christ and become a believer.

Personally, I find keeping all this straight in my head tiring, so I keep a prayer journal. Writing stuff down gives me a way to refer to what I vented during my *Ascent*. It also gives me a way of reviewing the past week, month, and even year. If journaling isn't your thing and you don't feel the need to hold on to any paper, jotting brief notes on a sticky-note or two could work. After you're done praying, you can toss them and move on.

The Holy Place is a powerful place to pray because we're far more likely to pray according to God's will. So make bold requests. As you pray, remember God has promised to be with you and provide for you. Pray with that in the front of your mind, infusing your faith with supernatural expectation.

The writer of the book of Hebrews says,

"We do not have a high priest who is unable to sympathize with our weaknesses, but we have one who has been tempted in every way, just as we are—yet was without sin. Let us then approach the throne of grace with confidence, so that we may receive mercy and grace in our time of need" (Hebrews 4:14-16).

Spirit-led prayer is prayer grounded in the gospel, informed by faith in God's character, promises, and word. It's prayer infused with Holy-Spirit insight, revelation, and confidence. This is the posture the Temple Pathway produces in us, so now we pray. Here are a few tips for your prayers.

Frame your requests with specific details so you can discern how and when they get answered. "Bless me," isn't a specific prayer. Even if God answered it, you might never connect the dots.

Second, stretch your faith! Ask for God-sized miracles. He is able to exceed everything we could ever ask or think (Ephesians 3:20,21).

When do you stop praying? The answer, for me at least, is simple: I pray until I can't think of anything else to pray about. I linger in prayer until God has released my heart from all confusion, anxiety, anger, frustration, guilt, shame, distraction, and concern.

If you remember another sin to confess, confess it and receive God's grace. If another issue comes up, talk to God about it and give it to him in prayer. If he brings up another issue, explore it. If he shares another scripture, study it. Keep going until there's nothing left. Until your mind and heart are at rest and full of him.

Yes, it's possible. And it's beautiful. Best of all, it prepares us for the climax of the entire Temple Pathway: the Holy of Holies.

Key points from this chapter:

- The Holy Place is a space of revelation and prayer.

- The showbread is the prophetic promise of God's never-ending faithfulness and provision. He will provide all our needs through Christ and his word.

- The lampstand reminds us to listen to the wisdom of the Holy Spirit so his insight can flow into every area of our lives to produce fruit.

- The altar of incense is a place of surrendered prayer, grounded in Christ's word and his promise of provision, guided by ongoing revelation from the Holy Spirit.

- Praying from the Holy Place is powerful. We are far more likely to pray according to God's will because he's transformed us through the Temple Pathway.

- **Q:** *What intrigues or excites you most about what you learned in this chapter, and why?*

- **Q:** *How has this chapter shaped your view of prayer? What are you going to do about it?*

11

The Holy of Holies

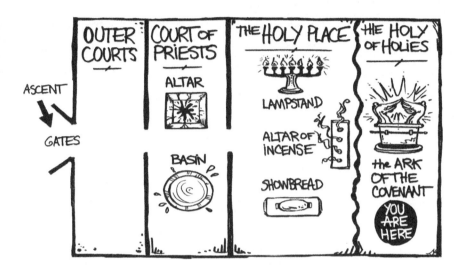

I began this book by saying that we can access God anywhere, at any time. And that's true. Unfortunately, we're usually full of ourselves when we turn to him. As a result, we often can't see, hear, experience, and enjoy him fully. Struggles, worries, frustrations, questions, conflicts, emotions, hormones, temptations, negative thoughts, terrible ideas... many days, we're a mess. And then we sit down and try to focus on God. Try to ignore all our issues. Try to be spiritual.

And fail. And fail. And give up on meaningful time with God.

Until now.

Have you ever been to a movie where some idiot in the theatre won't shut up? The guy won't stop moving. He keeps getting up to stretch. It drives you crazy, right? You can't enjoy the movie because his distraction is taking centre-stage. Eventually you lose it and bark out orders: "Down in front!"

Intimacy with God is like that. Your only hope for enjoying God is to process all the distracting junk on the front of your mind so he can take its place. Going with the Temple Pathway facilitates that "down in front" miracle. Once you settle your tangled brain, you're free to step into the Holy of Holies, where there's nothing—and no one—but God.

Every step we've unpacked in the Temple Pathway so far is biblical and necessary. We're commanded to pour out our hearts before God, to praise and thank him, to confess our sin and forgive others, and lay our requests before him with faith-filled expectation. But we're also invited to go "higher up and further in," to take the ultimate step of meeting with God face to face in the Holy of Holies.

I can tell you from experience: It's far too easy to get what I need from God, and unplug from my quiet time before marinating in the Holy of Holies. I'm like the kid who comes home from school and leaves a trail on the floor made of stinky shoes, books, lunch garbage, muddy footprints, plus a form my mom needs to sign by tomorrow. I stride right past her to snag a chocolate-chip cookie from the cookie jar, give her a peck on the cheek, bounce out of the kitchen and leave her standing there calling out, "Uh, I missed you too!"

Jesus died a gruesome death to give us life. One of the most staggering gifts that comes with that life is a mind-blowing treasure for our pleasure—the Holy of Holies. The Father wants us to get past our wants and needs to feast on him alone.

Knowing my self-centred tendencies, I don't consider my quiet time complete until I've spent at least a few minutes completely still before God with nothing on my mind but him. I've found that unless I bask in God's glory each day, I can't seem to live from my new self in Christ. Without that transcendent moment, my old self rears its ugly head far too quickly.

Here are some important things I've learned along the way about spending time in the Holy of Holies. I trust they'll be helpful to you as well.

Entering God's presence

God is everywhere, which means he's always here. We can access him anywhere. "Where can I go from your Spirit?" David asked. "Where can I flee from your presence? If I go up to the heavens, you are there; if I make my bed in the depths, you are there," (Psalm 139:7,8). Thank God!

Theologians call this God's omnipresence—his 'everywhere-ness.' But no human being has ever experienced God's omnipresence, because we aren't everywhere. We're somewhere—locked into a single time, space, and place. This is why nearly all references to God's presence in the scriptures describe how he manifests himself to people in time, space and place. Just because God is everywhere doesn't mean he never shows up somewhere.

Moses' relationship with God illustrates this truth in box-breaking ways. One day, the Lord said, "Go up to the land flowing with milk and honey. But I will not go with you" (Exodus 33:3).

Moses replied,

> "If your Presence does not go with us, do not send us up from here. How will anyone know that you are pleased with me and with your people unless you go with us? What else will distinguish me and your people from all the other people on the face of the earth?"

Moses knew God's presence *with* the Hebrews was more tangible (and miss-able!) than his omnipresence. Many believers fail to make this distinction and settle for less than God has for them.

Further, "The Lord would speak to Moses face to face, as one speaks to a friend" (Exodus 33:11). Moses clearly enjoyed a more intimate manifestation of God's presence than God being *with* the Hebrews in a general sense.

And it gets better! "Then the Lord said, "There is a place near me where you may stand on a rock. When my glory passes by, I will put you in a cleft in the rock and cover you with my hand until I have passed by" (Exodus 33:21,22). Moses experienced manifestations of God's presence that surpassed his face-to-face intimacy with him! This was so locked in to time, space and place that standing near a particular rock put Moses nearer to God. Let that break your brain; God comes and goes. He descends, ascends, moves, and even passes by.

This is important, because the New Testament urges us to "approach God's throne of grace with confidence" (Hebrews 4:16). We read:

> "Therefore, brothers and sisters, since we have confidence to enter the Most Holy Place by the blood of Jesus, by a new and living way opened for us through the curtain, his body, and since we have a great priest over the house of God, let us draw near to God with a sincere heart and with the full assurance that faith brings, having our hearts sprinkled to cleanse us from a guilty conscience and having our bodies washed with pure water. Let us hold unswervingly to the hope we profess, for he who promised is faithful." (Hebrews 10:20-23)

Drawing near to God is not metaphorical. We have greater access to God than just his omnipresence or even relational intimacy with him. We can go right in to experience God in the Holy of Holies. Yes, part of this is about making ourselves fully present to God, but he may also manifest more of his presence to us as we draw near to him. Oh, how I cherish these moments with my favourite person in the universe!

A dear friend of mine named Norm passed away in 2022. I miss him so much. Norm and I often met for coffee to talk about life, our kids, and Jesus. But my favourite thing to do with Norm, right until the end, was to spend time in God's presence together. Norm seemed to enter God's presence more effortlessly than anyone I've ever met. This wasn't just about Norm 'tuning in' to God. God also met with Norm.

As I visited Norm at his bedside in his final weeks, I would simply invite Jesus to come manifest his presence, then pray as the Spirit led me. Even as Norm's body wasted away, his spirit was fully alive. The best way to describe our experience is that we 'slipped into' the presence of God together. A tangible peace would fill the room.

Sometimes God's presence was so palpable that I opened my eyes expecting to see God's visible glory dancing around us. Instead, I would find Norm with his eyes closed, grinning ear to ear, tears spilling over his cheeks. His physical eyes may have closed under the weariness of illness, but his spiritual eyes were wide open as he gazed into the face of his beautiful Saviour.

Posture

The Holy of Holies is all about worship. Throughout the Bible, the word worship often means "to bow down before, to prostrate oneself before." And throughout biblical history, worshippers bowed—not just in their hearts, like we North Americans think is enough, but with their bodies. Throughout the Psalms, praise and worship is expressed through clapping, shouting, bowing, kneeling, and lifting our hands to God.

There's something humbling about this. There should be. Try it sometime. Then keep doing it. God is worthy.

Interestingly enough, King David never says, "Lord, I worship you with my hands in my pockets." Moses never writes, "Praise the Lord by checking your phone." No one ever says, "God is worthy, but I don't have to show it on the outside." Romans 12:1 says, "I urge you, brothers and sisters, in view of God's mercy, to offer your *bodies* as a living sacrifice, holy and pleasing to God—this is your true and proper worship."

There is a fascinating relationship between our bodies and our souls. To illustrate this, I like to guide people through an exercise in expression. I'll instruct a volunteer to stand and pray the first thing that comes to mind. Next, I have them open their palms to God, looking up to heaven, and pray again. Next, I have them lift their hands—once again, praying the first thing that comes to mind. I follow this up with kneeling, and finally lying prostrate (face to the ground).

What's interesting is that each posture prompts a different prayer. Palms-up postures tend to inspire "I need you" or "I receive" prayers. Hands-up postures prompt praise and thanksgiving. Kneeling imbues us with a sense of humility or dependence. And prostrating ourselves instills a sense of God's greatness and our smallness. Don't kid yourself; your posture matters!

I love to bow down before God. Like, flat on the floor. Prostrating myself before him reminds me of his hugeness. I'm struck again by my utter dependence on his grace and mercy.

If you never feel the urge to face plant in the Holy of Holies, you may have pride issues to process.

Imagination

Depending on the church tradition you grew up in, you may feel wary of the word *imagination.* For some, it conjures the idea of 'make-believe.' For others, imagination is associated with counterfeit New Age practices that lead us astray.

There are some legitimate concerns baked into those fears. The devil is real. The Apostle Paul wrote, "I am afraid that just as Eve was deceived by the serpent's cunning, your minds may somehow be led astray from your sincere and pure devotion to Christ" (2 Corinthians 11:3). Because that's true, God is never offended when we exercise biblical discernment.

Some people think the purpose of testing the spirits is to discern the devil and his counterfeits. It's not. That's a trap, because we always get more of what we focus on! John clearly instructs us to "test the spirits to see *whether they are from God*" (I John 4:4, *emphasis mine*). The purpose of true discernment is to find "the God-stuff" so we can run with it. Paul also said, "Hate what is evil; cling to what is good" (Romans 12:9). The same is true with our imagination.

It might be helpful to realize that the word 'imagination' isn't just referring to one thing. The Merriam-Webster definition of *imagination* includes six senses of the word:

1. The act or power of forming a mental image of something not present to the senses or never before wholly perceived in reality

2. Creative ability

3. Ability to confront and deal with a problem

4. The thinking or active mind

5. A creation of the mind

6. Fanciful or empty assumption

It's clear that God has imbued human beings with "a thinking or active mind." This includes "creative ability" (as those created in the image of our Creator). We can also "confront and deal with problems." But imagination also includes "the act or power of forming a mental image of something not present to the senses or never before wholly perceived in reality." This is the sense of the word that comes in handy for prayer.

Yes, it's true that some of our thoughts are simply "a creation of the mind" or just "fanciful or empty assumptions." We can imagine a pink elephant, for example. We're exceptionally good at worrying about things that may never happen, or assuming people's motives are bad when they offend us. Our minds really are capable of fantasy, and the devil takes advantage of these tendencies. But "forming a mental image of something not present to the senses" isn't New Age; it's human.

Are you sitting down? Good. Close your eyes, and imagine the chair you're sitting on. Is that fantasy, or is it simply visualizing the truth? Now recall the last conversation you had with someone close to you. Replay it in your mind. Is that "make believe" or a genuine memory?

Imagination is a gift from God and a vital part of a vibrant faith. Listen to what Oswald Chambers says in his treasure-laden devotional, *My Utmost For His Highest*:

> "If your imagination is starved, do not look back to your own experience; it is God Whom you need. Go right out of yourself, away from the face of your idols, away from everything that has been starving your imagination. Rouse yourself, take the gibe that Isaiah gave the people, and deliberately turn your imagination to God." One of the reasons of stultification in prayer is that there is no imagination, no power of putting ourselves deliberately before God."

When Jesus says, "I am the Vine, you are the branches," he's trying to stir our imaginations to visualize what he's saying. This is true of all symbolism and imagery throughout the scriptures. Through the act of visualization, we come to see, hear, feel, and experience the reality of his words.

I should mention here that it's quite possible to be deceived by the devil or misled by our own desires and thoughts. In John chapter ten, Jesus warns us against the influence of strangers, thieves, and wolves (John 10:5,8,12). Christ provides a decisive victory tactic for each of those influences. The point of his teaching is to produce confidence in him, not to paralyze us with fear of the enemy.

Biblical discernment is really quite simple. When we're engaged in a spiritual experience, we can simply reject anything that is not in perfect alignment with God's word and the character and person of the Lord Jesus Christ. God commands us to test things so we can give ourselves more fully to the good things he's sharing with us. Discernment doesn't just protect us from being 'taken in' by deception. It prevents us from *missing out* on genuine God encounters.

Prayer journaling our experiences with God is an important part of this process. We can circle back to things we thought we heard God say to test the fruit of those encounters. If the word we received was predictive, we can see whether it actually happened. If it felt like a stretch theologically, we can hold it up to the word of God to determine whether it is biblically sound.

Remember where we started in this simple book: learning how to interact with God. Our God-given envisioning—especially when it's been purified by the Temple Pathway—can become a precious encounter with him. As the late, beloved teacher Leanne Payne wrote in her beautiful book, *The Healing Presence* (p. 146);

> "The symbolic mind, working properly, brings together head and heart. What starts out as a deliberate visualizing of the cross becomes an intuition of the real. God sends His healing grace, a thing we could never have deliberately visualized."

That's it exactly; I begin by visualizing something true and biblical, including him in the picture. Sometimes, even often, what I'm seeing begins taking on a life of its own. I'm no longer 'in charge' because the Spirit of God has taken the wheel. In these moments, I don't know where things are going. I'm often surprised by what unfolds. Discernment should always be in play, but I don't let fleshly fear bind my imaginative powers in restrictive chains that God never intended for them.

In his fascinating book, *Can You Hear Me*, Brad Jersak relates a profound story told by Archbishop Bloom: "Once the Curé d'Ars, a French saint of the eighteenth century, asked an old peasant what he was doing sitting for hours in the church, seemingly not even praying; the peasant replied, 'I look at him, he looks at me and we are happy together.'"

The most profound moments of my life occur when I fix my eyes on Jesus and see him gazing back at me. His eyes are as rich as galaxies, radiant as stars, formidable as a thunderstorm, playful as a pup, soft as a doe. Sometimes my vision of him is so clear that I am both undone and remade at the same time. In the stillness of each other's presence, we simply enjoy each other, and it's glorious.

I regularly ask God to open the eyes and ears of my heart during my Temple Pathway. It helps to imagine myself walking through the Temple, stepping across the threshold from the Holy Place into the Holy of Holies. Sometimes, I pray Moses' simple prayer: "Show me your glory" (Exodus 33:18).

God loves to take hold of our imaginations and fill them with himself, stretching us in ways we never dreamed possible:

> "Now to him who is able to do immeasurably more than all we ask or imagine, according to his power that is at work within us, to him be glory in the church and in Christ Jesus throughout all generations, for ever and ever! Amen" (Ephesians 3:20,21).

If you need help to envision God's presence like this, meditate on some key scripture passages. Try Isaiah chapter 6, or Revelation chapters 1 and 4 to get you started. The throne room in heaven is the spiritual equivalent of the Holy of Holies on earth, but infinitely more awesome. One day, our imagination won't be necessary. Until then, God meets us there.

Feeling it... or not

I'm not usually overwhelmed with emotion in the Holy of Holies. Sometimes my joy is euphoric—but the most common sensation for me is a simple peace and a sense that I am centred in Christ. I'm with him, he's with me, and it's enough.

In the same way, it's relatively rare for me to feel God physically. But that's okay. Feeling God is not the point. Worshipping him is. Remember our goal as we interact with God: not that we would get something out of him, but that he would get more out of us.

What to do in the Holy of Holies

I'm often fresh out of prayer requests in the Holy of Holies. There are no conflicts, just God's eternal glory. Awe of Jesus has quieted my questions. My worries have given way to worship. There isn't a whole lot of doing—just being and becoming.

The Temple Pathway frees us to forget ourselves in the presence of God. It releases us to do what the Westminster Confession asserts is the chief end of man: to "enjoy God and glorify him forever."

I often envision God waiting for me to show up in the Holy of Holies. He likes to fill my imagination with an image of his glory—dancing flames, blinding light, liquid love, or electricity. I often get a visual image of God's power reaching out to me, engulfing me, filling me, or healing me. When that happens, I worship him even more. Interestingly enough, I don't think I've ever 'seen' the same thing twice.

Sometimes I speak words of prayer and worship. Other times, I just behold him and revel in his awesomeness. I love to focus on aspects of his character—his holiness, his beauty, his love, his perfection.

Another great tip, one I borrowed from writer and speaker Mark Virkler: When you step into God's presence, *smile*. Like, physically smile. It will change the posture of your heart. We know that because of his great love for us, and through Jesus, the Father is smiling on us, too. That's not just a figurative thing, by the way.

Finally, saints throughout the eons have discovered music is a powerful worship aid. But make sure the song you're using at this point in the Temple Pathway is a 'Holy of Holies' song. We focus most church music on other elements of the flow—Ascent, thanksgiving, the cross, and prayer requests. True worship music addresses God personally vs. just talking about him. It's focused mostly on who God is, not just what he can do for us.

Now what?

When the saints of scripture met with God like this—face to face—the stress they came with often evaporated so they could "go in peace." This wasn't because all their issues were resolved, but because their mountain became a molehill in the presence of God. Even poor Job experienced this reality. He lost everything he held dear in waves of devastating tragedy, but when God showed up and revealed his glory, his heart softened and began to heal. When we're lost in God's awesomeness, we tend to forget what was so all-consuming a few minutes earlier.

God made us to worship. If you've gone with the flow of the Temple Pathway, you'll be able to worship without your own issues distracting your mind and obscuring your view of his glory. But there's one more blessing to embrace, one so mind-bendingly fantastic that it almost seems blasphemous to believe. Are you ready? God isn't the only one seated in the heavenly throne room: *You are.*

> "God raised us up with Christ and seated us with him in
> the heavenly realms in Christ Jesus, in order that in the

coming ages he might show the incomparable riches of his grace, expressed in his kindness to us in Christ Jesus." (Ephesians 2:6,7)

"Since, then, you have been raised with Christ, set your hearts on things above, where Christ is, seated at the right hand of God. Set your minds on things above, not on earthly things." (Colossians 3:1,2)

Not only is this true, it's foundational. The gospel is clear: The only way you can stand firm for Jesus on earth is to sit firmly with Jesus in heaven. We must all answer God's call to take our seat with him in the heavenly places. Seated with Christ, we rest in his finished work and live from heaven to earth. Surrounded by God's riches in glory, we understand he "has blessed us in the heavenly realms with every spiritual blessing in Christ" (Ephesians 1:3).

Learning to live from our heavenly seat changes how we see every situation we face. We pray from super-abundance, not lack. We face challenges from victory instead of defeat. Seated with Christ, every enemy, trial, and temptation is beneath our feet because Christ has put it there (Ephesians 1:22,23). Only God is worthy of worship, but rejecting or ignoring this astounding gift robs him of glory and locks us into earth-bound religion devoid of his power.

Another common result of taking our seat with God in the Holy of Holies is a renewed sense of clarity and call. We approach him with what's on our mind, but we leave enraptured by what's on his. The Lord commissioned Isaiah from this most Holy Place. John received a powerful vision, what we now call the book of Revelation—and an assignment to share it with the rest of the world. Even lepers and demoniacs left on a mission after meeting with Jesus.

The most important to-do list in my life is made from the fresh marching orders I receive before the throne. One day, while I was basking in God's holiness, he said, "Get up, son, and go bless someone." So I did, sending a heartfelt text to encourage a friend. The joy of Jesus flowed through me like a mighty river. Remember, we're all priests of God's presence now. Our mission is to help others get right with God through Jesus Christ. That's what priests do.

If your time with Jesus never moves you to reach out to others, something is wrong. The Holy Spirit is empowering you and infusing you with his great heart. The Father is "not wanting anyone to perish, but everyone to come to repentance" (II Peter 3:9). Jesus "came to seek and save the lost" (Luke 19:10), and stated plainly that "where I am, my servant will also be" (John 12:26). The more God gets ahold of us, the more our heart will beat with and break for what breaks his.

If you'd like to explore greater depths of God's presence, check out <u>my message on YouTube</u>. If you're reading a paper copy of this book, scan this QR code:

Key points from this chapter:

• It's far too easy to get what we need from God and unplug from our quiet time without marinating in the Holy of Holies first.

• The Father wants us to get past our wants and needs to feast on him alone.

• What we do with our bodies—our physical posture before God—shapes what our minds and hearts both give and receive from him.

• Imagination is a gift from God. As he opens the eyes of our hearts, we can visualize him and his truth, which may lead to greater encounters with him.

• God is not offended when we test the spirits. He's counting on it.

• Feeling God is not the point. Worshipping him is.

• When we come into God's presence, it actually helps to smile. God wants to spend time with us, mutually enjoying each-other's company.

• Q: *Have you ever spent time in the Holy of Holies before? If so, what was it like?*

• *Have you ever given your imagination to God, to fill with his truth and glory? Why or why not?*

• Q: *If not, how has this Temple Pathway helped you step deeper into God's presence?*

• Q: *Is there anything holding you back or causing you to doubt what God has available to us in Christ? Explain.*

12

After the Amen

Congratulations! You've just walked through the Temple Pathway, a powerful framework created by God and fulfilled by Christ that helps you:

- Grow intimacy with him

- Embrace and apply the gospel of Jesus to every area of your life

- Process your life journey with God so you can become more like Jesus over time

- Grow in nine key spiritual practices for your walk with God: *Ascent, Thanksgiving, Praise, Heart-Check, Confession, Giving and Receiving Grace, hearing God, Spirit-inspired prayer, and Worship.*

The beauty of the Temple Pathway is that it weaves all these elements into a memorable and repeatable pathway that unfolds in five distinct steps: *Ascent*, the *Outer Courts*, The *Court of Priests*, the *Holy Place*, and the *Holy of Holies*. Each of these practices are portable. Once you learn a practice, you can step into it any time, depending on what's needed.

If you blow it during the day, don't wait to confess your sin during your devotions. Do it on the spot! When God answers a prayer, thank and praise him for it immediately. If you're feeling stressed, step into the

Holy Place. Remind yourself of God's promise of presence and provision in Christ. See the wisdom and power flowing into that situation, and pray with that empowering mindset. If you have a spare moment, step into the Holy of Holies to worship God and rest in him. The elements of the flow are ingredients for intimacy that can infuse every situation we face with his grace and power.

But the Temple Pathway isn't dummy-proof, so let me warn you about a few common traps to avoid.

Missing the point

The tabernacle and Temple were God's gift to humanity, but a funny thing happened along the way to the New Testament: The Hebrews missed the whole point.

Over time, the Temple rituals *became* the goal. The elements became the end instead of a means to an end. The flow is supposed to lead you closer to Jesus. Walking through the Temple Pathway isn't supposed to become a set of rules. It's supposed to saturate our entire lives with Christ and his gospel.

When my kids first started learning to ride a bike, we slapped training wheels on the sides. The training wheels freed them to learn the strange dance of pedalling, turning, braking, and balance with a healthy fear of falling.

I'll never forget the day we took off our son Noah's training wheels. I set him up for success with his bum on the seat, feet on the pedals. My job was to hold on to the back of the bike and run behind him until he was ready for me to let go.

"Okay, buddy," I explained. "What I want you to do is start pedalling, but don't work—"

Wheeee!

Before I could stop him, he took off. I mean, he pedalled the bike right out of my hands and just... rode the thing. My jaw dropped as I watched my Noah bob, weave, and pump his way down the sidewalk without the training wheels. Without *me*.

He was free!

Yes, he wiped out eventually. But that didn't matter anymore. He was too thrilled to become discouraged by a scraped elbow. Noah had experienced the rhythm and momentum of riding a bike, felt the wind in his hair, and tasted big-boy freedom. Eventually, he learned he didn't even need to pedal the whole time to stay upright. He could glide, skid, pop wheelies, and kathunk over curbs.

Your experience with God can be like that.

Your quiet time is your bike, and the Temple Pathway is your training wheels. Your relationship with God must grow beyond the routines we use to keep us on track. He'll use it to soften your heart to him, so he can get to you anywhere, at any time. Once you taste the freedom, you'll never depend on devotional books again.

Even though the nine spiritual practices have become a regular part of my life, I still use the Temple Pathway in my quiet times. I've found that my time with God becomes unbalanced pretty quickly if I don't walk the path. I still find walking through the entire flow helps me give myself more fully to God in those disciplines. I also need to grow in the Holy Place and Holy of Holies practices—especially Spirit-inspired prayer, and worship.

This brings us back full-circle to our relationship goals. A 'home-run' quiet time is one where I'm more fully given over to Jesus after the amen. And how do I know I'm more fully his? Remember "the big four." A successful daily devotion time means I've given God:

- My full attention
- My deepest affection

- My ongoing dependence
- My obedience to his will

The 'only way'?

After experiencing the power of going with the Temple Pathway we might be tempted to think it's the only way to spend time with God. We might even make it a rule or even a law and judge ourselves and others based on that law. That would be missing the point, too. There is nothing in scripture that commands us to use the Temple Pathway the way I've outlined it. There is no black and white bible verse that rates our relationship with God based on how well or how often we use it.

What we have in scripture is a personal invitation from God to approach him in a God-ordained way, custom-designed to help us thrive. It's up to us to learn how to ride our quiet time bike with joy, to learn the spiritual rhythms we'll need to walk with Christ for the rest of our lives.

At first, your quiet time will benefit from pedalling to a clear routine. Routines help us find our rhythm. But once you discover that rhythm, be careful: routines can easily become life-sucking ruts.

Once you've learned to ride the Temple Pathway bike, you won't forget how. You may get rusty, but within a few minutes after dusting it off, you'll be sailing along again with little effort—and *a lot* of joy.

The 'quiet time script' trap

Going with the Temple Pathway is a path, not a script. It gives us direction, not directions. In fact, if you're being real with God, every single quiet time will play out differently.

Some days, your opening line is going to be, "I'm so sorry I lost my temper." Other days, the first thing on your mind might be something you're thankful for, or something about God you want to praise him for.

Sometimes I lead with something from scripture that's already on my mind. Sometimes the Temple elements happen as they happen. Don't get locked into a script. Go with the flow.

Give God permission to be original with you. If you're actually connecting with God instead of going through the motions, he's going to speak, guide, and lead you in unique ways. No two encounters with the living God in scripture played out the same. Why would it be any different with us?

Most days, my venting, thanksgiving, and praise kind of meld together. I often start with thanksgiving. Sometimes God is teaching me something before I do anything else.

Jesus is in charge. If he wants to spend an hour unpacking a Bible passage with you, go with it. If he wants you to be still and know that he is God, be still. If you feel drawn to worship before you 'get to' the Holy of Holies, fall to your knees and do it. If you're in the Holy of Holies and he reminds you of a sin you've committed, confess it!

One day as began my *Ascent,* the Holy Spirit prompted me to play a familiar worship song on my laptop instead. In my mind's eye I was drawn into the throne room almost immediately, where I experienced a beautiful vision of God.

A guy I know related how when he was sitting in the Holy of Holies one day, he became so peaceful that he fell asleep. He felt guilty about nodding off, but I thought it was awesome. What a beautiful thing it is to fall asleep in the arms of the Father! The Temple Pathway isn't about the order. It's about the intimacy. Divinely inspired variety keeps the Temple Pathway fresh day after day.

In Psalm 23, David reflects on the rich variety he experienced throughout his spiritual journey.

First, he framed it all by declaring, "The Lord is my shepherd. I won't lack anything." He knew if God was leading him, he'd always get what he needed to be faithful, no matter where the trail led. Sometimes

God led him to lie down in green pastures. Other times, the Lord invited him to drink from quiet streams. Other times he found himself following God through dark valleys or fighting enemies in dangerous battles. But through it all, his cup overflowed. He knew he would dwell in God's presence forever (see Psalm 23).

David understood that relationship with God is about rhythms, not routines. And certainly not scripts.

The 'checklist' trap

After experiencing the power in each of the Temple Pathway elements, you may be tempted to think of your quiet time as a series of things you need to get done. While it's certainly good for us to experience all the elements along the pathway, your time with God is not a checklist.

Ascent? Check.

Thanksgiving? Check.

Forgiveness? Check.

Surrendered prayer? Oops, forgot that one. Sorry, God.

Going with the Temple Pathway isn't about checking things off a list so we can feel good about ourselves. It's not about "Devotional correctness." It's about walking with Jesus in all of life.

Some people view their quiet time itself as something to check off a daily to-do list. *There, I did my God time. Now I can get on with the rest of my day.* But remember, the Temple Pathway helps us live our entire lives saturated, empowered, and guided by God. It's not something to "get done." We're like little fish swimming ever deeper into the kingdom river. God's current will take us where we need to go.

As my son Noah learned, pedalling our bike *consistently* is important. He also discovered that pedalling *constantly* misses the point. The point is movement—getting from A to B. And just like bike riding, the fun part is gliding, weaving, and improvising.

When I ride my bike, I love cresting a hill after pumping hard, sitting back and enjoying the breeze as momentum carries me forward. The key is knowing when to pedal, how hard to pedal, and when to relax and enjoy the ride. It's the same with your relationship with God.

When you do the same thing over and over again, it eventually gets old. So ditch the checklist.

The 'all or nothing' trap

When I unpacked this Temple Pathway in our small group, one of my friends said, "This is great, but I just don't have the time to do this every day." She's up early, home late, often brings work home, and has a husband to love. How could she possibly find the time to meander through each element of the flow during such a busy schedule? The temptation? Reject the Temple Pathway entirely.

I have two suggestions to avoid falling into this trap.

First, every moment you spend loving God with your attention and affection counts. Something is better than nothing. Do what you can with what you have, and grow from there. My challenge to my friend was simple: *What if you set apart time for this once this coming week?* She nodded; Once, she could do.

Maybe you could sit down with God for little snippets during the week, then go 'long and deep' on Sunday morning before church. I highly recommend finding at least one day a week where you can relax into the Temple Pathway and let it take as long as it needs to. God will guide you into a rhythm that's right for you.

Second, this doesn't have to take two hours. The Temple Pathway includes a lot of elements, but once you learn them they'll come naturally to you. Some days, I spend over an hour immersed in the flow. Other days I'm out in twenty minutes. You could do this in *five* minutes if need be! In fact, the last chapter frames out a "Five-Minute Flow" and a "Fifteen-Minute Flow" for you to try. That may be the best place to start if the thought of extended quiet times intimidates you. Sometimes I go 'long and deep' in the morning, and then catch a few 'Fives' throughout my day.

Final thought: Further and Deeper

You'll recall that "When Christ came as high priest...He went through the greater and more perfect tabernacle that is not man-made, that is to say, not a part of this creation" (Hebrews 9:11). God patterned the earthly tabernacle and Temple after a spiritual, heavenly tabernacle that's available to us today.

The prophet Ezekiel recorded an exquisitely detailed vision of a prophetic Temple spanning six full chapters in his book (Ezekiel 40-46). The scale and size of the Temple in his vision dwarfed Herod's Temple, which occupied the square footage equivalent to four American football fields! Ezekiel's description involves meticulous measurement of every conceivable dimension in the Temple layout. Remember, we measure what matters—and the same is true of God. This is why we've spent so much time exploring the Temple within this book.

After the Temple's inner measurements were complete, the angel guiding Ezekiel's vision led him outside, where he pointed out "water... trickling from the south side" (Ezekiel 47:2). He wanted Ezekiel to experience the power of what would flow from the Temple. The picture is stunning:

> "As the man went eastward with a measuring line in his
> hand, he measured off a thousand cubits and then led

me through water that was ankle-deep. He measured off another thousand cubits and led me through water that was knee-deep. He measured off another thousand and led me through water that was up to the waist. He measured off another thousand, but now it was a river that I could not cross, because the water had risen and was deep enough to swim in—a river that no one could cross. He asked me, "Son of man, do you see this?"

"Then he led me back to the bank of the river. When I arrived there, I saw a great number of trees on each side of the river. He said to me, "This water flows toward the eastern region and goes down into the Arabah, where it enters the Dead Sea.

"When it empties into the sea, the salty water there becomes fresh. Swarms of living creatures will live wherever the river flows. There will be large numbers of fish, because this water flows there and makes the salt water fresh; so where the river flows everything will live.

Fishermen will stand along the shore; from En Gedi to En Eglaim there will be places for spreading nets. The fish will be of many kinds—like the fish of the Mediterranean Sea. But the swamps and marshes will not become fresh; they will be left for salt. Fruit trees of all kinds will grow on both banks of the river. Their leaves will not wither, nor will their fruit fail. Every month they will bear fruit, because the water from the sanctuary flows to them. Their fruit will serve for food and their leaves for healing." (Ezekiel 47:3-12).

Theologians still debate the precise meaning of this vision, but several things are perfectly clear. One, the vision refers to the Temple

Jesus fulfilled and empowered through his death and resurrection. Ezekiel's vision illustrates what the gospel makes possible.

Two, the increasing flow of water from the Temple illustrates the life and power of the Holy Spirit that can grow and flow from our experience of the gospel. Again, that's why I wrote this book.

Three, the Holy Spirit's flow can affect the world around us in profound ways. Where the rivers flows, life blooms. Even people living downstream from our lives can taste and see the fruit of our walk with God.

Four, depth increases with distance. The angel was using what's called a 'long cubit' for his measurements—which amounts to a long, purposeful step. For the first thousand cubits, the flow didn't increase much. But after four thousand strides, it had swelled into an uncrossable river. The depth of your experience and impact depends on how you walk this out.

Are you willing to take long, purposeful steps? To stride forward every day, day after day, until you've put in a thousand steps with God? How about two thousand? Or four? Are you willing to make this a way of life? I've logged sixty-two prayer journals over thirty-five years, spending time with God nearly every day since 1988. That's 12,775 'steps.' It's not about earning God's blessing. It's just that there is no substitute for walking with God over a lifetime.

Five, your relationship with God is meant to bless and empower others. Intimacy with God creates an overflow. The promise is powerful: "where the river flows everything will live" (Ezekiel 47:9).

And finally, the heavenly flow of worship you've been using hasn't just been guiding you through a bunch of mental exercises. It's been ushering you deeper into God himself. His gates open up regular experience with him. The Court of Priests invites us deeper into his grace. God's Holy Place draws us deeper into his wisdom. The Holy of Holies saturates us with God's glory. "In him we live and move and have our being" (Acts 17:28). If you haven't jumped in already, it's time to go with the flow.

In my Bible, Revelation 22 begins with a wondrous heading: *Eden Restored.* Watch how the fulfillment of Ezekiel's vision will unfold one day:

> "Then the angel showed me the river of the water of life, as clear as crystal, flowing from the throne of God and of the Lamb down the middle of the great street of the city. On each side of the river stood the tree of life, bearing twelve crops of fruit, yielding its fruit every month. And the leaves of the tree are for the healing of the nations. No longer will there be any curse. The throne of God and of the Lamb will be in the city, and his servants will serve him. They will see his face, and his name will be on their foreheads. There will be no more night. They will not need the light of a lamp or the light of the sun, for the Lord God will give them light. And they will reign for ever and ever" (Revelation 22:1-5).

The Temple is our blueprint, our pathway, our flow of worship, our destiny. And destiny awaits.

Key points from this chapter:

• The nine spiritual practices we learn through the Temple Pathway are 'portable.' Once we learn them, we can step into them at a moment's notice throughout the day, depending on what's needed.

• **Q:** *Can you recall the five spaces in the Temple Pathway? What are they? Try it now.*

• The Temple Pathway isn't the point; interacting with God, becoming more fully his, and growing intimacy with him are the point.

• We should be careful not to get so wrapped up in doing the Temple Pathway 'correctly' that we rehearse it like a script that robs us of real intimacy.

• The Temple Pathway is not a checklist that God expects us to complete each day.

• The Temple Pathway is not an 'all-or-nothing' proposition. Any time spent interacting with God is important.

• **Q:** *Have you fallen into any of the pitfalls listed in this chapter? Why or why not?*

• Every quiet time unfolds differently because life is always changing, and God will lead us to lean into different elements during those changing seasons.

• There are 'short' versions of the Temple Pathway we can engage in, but we should aim to 'go long and deep' at least once per week.

• *Q:* *When will you take time to practice the Five-Minute Flow... today?*

- *Q: If you haven't figured it out already, when will you book off time to walk through the whole Temple Flow with God?*

- *Q: Are you willing to put in your steps to create a rich history with God? Why or why not?*

Part Three:
Crash Courses

13

When life is busy

Throughout this book we've sunk our roots deep into the riches of the Temple Pathway. Ideally, we'd love to take our time with Jesus in each sacred space every single day. That said, there are days or even seasons when we will find this difficult. The better we understand the major beats of the Temple Pathway, the more portable it becomes for us. With that in mind, let's summarize the Temple Pathway as clearly and simply as possible.

Ascent: Vent what's on your mind and heart to God, no holding back.

Gates and Outer Courts: Thank God for his active role in your recent experience, then **praise** him for what this says about his character.

Court of Priests:

(1) **Heart Check:** Ask God to reveal what grieved his heart, quenched his work, and pleased him.

(2) **Confess** your sins and agree with him about what he reveals.

(3) Receive God's grace and listen for his **Affirmations** about what pleased his heart.

The Holy Place:

(1) Meditate on God's **word** and review God's **promises** in Christ.

(2) Listen for the Holy Spirit's **wisdom/revelation** about what you shared in your **Ascent.**

(3) **Pray** to the Father, grounded in Christ and his word and guided by the Holy Spirit.

The Holy of Holies: Focus on God and his presence, **worshiping** him for his greatness and glory.

Next, I'll share three Temple Pathway options you can use anytime, anywhere. Note that the short versions may not include every element but preserve the general flow.

THE TWO-MINUTE FLOW

The Two-Minute Flow is perfect for processing a single issue with God. It could go something like this:

> "Lord, You can see I'm really stressed about my work relationship with Bob. He's been so frustrating lately, and I feel so out of control in this situation (**Ascent**).
>
> Thank-You for giving me wisdom and grace for this struggle (**Thanksgiving**). You are my Counsellor and Guide, Holy Spirit (**Praise**).
>
> Lord God, please shine your light on me. How am I grieving your heart or quenching your work in this? (**Heart Check**). I'm sorry for treating him with disrespect and anger (**Confession**).
>
> Jesus, You've always been with me, through every moment of my life, You are with me now, and You will

be with me, no matter how this turns out (**Reviewing God's word/promises**).

Holy Spirit, would you guide me into truth on this? What would you like me to know about this situation? What am I missing? (**Hearing God**).

Father, I'm reminded now that Bob is going through a hard time at home right now, and he needs Jesus. Would you please give me grace for him? Help me to be a source of encouragement instead of conflict in his life. In Jesus' name, amen (**Spirit-led prayer**).

Then sit a moment, soaking in God's presence, glorifying Him (**Worship**).

THE FIVE-MINUTE FLOW

The "Five-Minute Flow" is ideal for giving your soul a 'reset' with God when you have a few minutes between activities during your day. You can use this as a rough guide:

- Vent one or two things on your mind right now to God.

- Thank God for his active role in two current things in your life.

- Praise him for what this says about who he is to you.

- Ask the Holy Spirit if there's anything he'd like to speak to you about (positive or negative) in your life, attitude, or actions right now.

- Confess (agree with him) about what he brings up.

- Verbally renounce (reject) any sinful beliefs or attitudes behind what you confess.

- Thank God for his faithfulness, and ask him if there is anything he wants you to know about what you vented earlier.

- Put this insight into action with brief prayers for those issues.
- Sit a moment, soaking in God's presence, glorifying him.

THE FIFTEEN-MINUTE FLOW

The "Fifteen-Minute Flow" provides a great 'mini-devotions' format when life is busy but you have a little time to sit with God. You can use this as a rough guide:

- Vent 2-3 things on your mind right now to God.
- Thank God for his active role in 2-3 current things in your life.
- Praise him for what this says about who he is to you.
- Ask the Holy Spirit if there is anything he'd like to speak to you about (positive or negative) in your life, attitude, or actions right now.
- Confess (agree with him) about what he brings up.
- Verbally renounce (reject) any sinful beliefs or attitudes behind what you confess, and ask him to fill you with his Spirit to live like Jesus.
- Thank God for his faithfulness in your life—past, present, and future.
- Reflect on a verse or two of scripture, conversing with the Holy Spirit about what you see, hear, and need to do about it.
- Ask the Holy Spirit if there is anything he wants you to know about what you vented earlier. Put this insight into action with brief prayers for those issues.
- Sit still, soaking in God's presence, glorifying him.

Get access to the toolbox

Would you like to grab PDFs of *all* the exercises and diagrams found in this book? You can find them here:

14

Bible Study Basics

The Christian life is built on the written word of God. As we already learned, God's word is our daily bread. Every believer in Jesus needs to commit to the life-long journey of Bible study and meditation.

There are many helpful Bible study resources and courses out there that can equip you to study the Bible. People spend their entire lives learning to study it effectively! That said, Bible study basics are really quite simple. My approach towards Bible study is to let the Bible tell us how to study it.

First things first

The Bible is a sixty-six book anthology that records God's interaction with humanity over thousands of years of history. This epic book of narrative, poetry, instruction, and prophecy traces the greatest love story ever told: God's pursuit of humanity through his plan of salvation.

"All scripture is God breathed" (II Timothy 3:16). The Bible is his written word to us, the voice of God in print. As such it carries his authority to inspire us, challenge us, and change us. Where I disagree with the Bible, I'm wrong.

Second, the scriptures point to Jesus and help us love and trust him for all of life (John 5:39,40). If you miss Jesus in your study, you've missed the point. Without a gospel foundation, you'll use the Bible to live your best life instead of being shaped by Jesus for God's purposes. A gospel-centred life frees us from the seduction of self-help strategies that produce our own righteousness, peace, and productivity. Anything built purely on my self-effort is a me-centred religion. It cannot save, heal, or deliver anyone or anything.

What about me?

Living a gospel-centred life does not mean Jesus is the only person we need to see in our Bible study. The Apostle James gives us the most concise crash course in Bible study you'll find anywhere:

> "Do not merely listen to the word, and so deceive yourselves. Do what it says. Anyone who listens to the word but does not do what it says is like a man who looks at his face in a mirror and, after looking at himself, goes away and immediately forgets what he looks like. But the man who looks intently into the perfect law that gives freedom, and continues to do this, not forgetting what he has heard, but doing it—he will be blessed in what he does" (James 1:22-25).

James uses variations of three verbs in this passage: Look, listen, and do. Here they are, in all their forms:

Looks, looking, looks, looks.

Listen, listens, heard.

Do, do, do, do, doing, does.

That's pretty clear.

When you study, *look,* James says. And keep looking—"intently," no less. That means infusing our intention with intensity.

What are we looking so intently for? James spells it out: "what it says." Not what we want it to say, or what we wish it said, but *what it says*. Pay attention to the flow of the passage, zooming out to surrounding verses to discern its context. What was the intent of the original author? What was he trying to communicate?

The intention or motivation we bring to our Bible Study exerts a massive influence on what we see in scripture. If we come looking to validate who we are and what we already believe, we may just find it—even if we're in the wrong. Human beings have a knack for twisting truth to make it bend to their preconceptions. Similarly, if we come to learn something, we probably will. Unfortunately, information does not equal transformation.

What intention should we bring to our Bible study? I recommend the relationship goal we set earlier in this book: *to give ourselves more fully to God.*

Here we return to 'the big four:' Offering God our full attention, our deepest affection, our dependence, and our obedience. We want to answer God's big questions with a resounding YES! *Do we trust him?* And *do we love him?* When I read my Bible, I'm primarily looking for how I can give myself more fully to God through my faith in Christ. I'm looking for ways my soul is out of alignment with God so I can let him bring me into harmony with his great heart.

So *look.* And according to James, don't stop looking until you see yourself in the stories and teachings you're looking at. It's like beholding yourself *in the mirror,* James says. Our personal transformation hinges on seeing ourselves reflected in God's word as vividly as possible and doing something about it. The Bible is the world's most accurate mirror. Without that self-revelation, we continually deceive ourselves.

Some popular preachers reject this idea, claiming the Bible is not about us at all. I've even heard some teachers scold their congregations out of trying to see themselves in the text!

That's not what the Bible teaches. When we see ourselves in God's word, it exposes "the thoughts and intentions of (our) heart" (Hebrews 4:12). Without this self-revelation, our thoughts and intentions go unchallenged by God's word.

Paul tells Timothy that "all Scripture is God-breathed and is useful for teaching, rebuking, correcting and training in righteousness so that the servant of God may be thoroughly equipped for every good work." (II Timothy 3:16,17). Who is being corrected and trained? Me! If we don't see ourselves in what we're reading, we won't be convicted by it. We must look for what we lack. We need the rebuke of God's Spirit and his correcting guidance in order to be equipped by his word.

What about the Bible stories we read? Yes, these characters are flawed types and shadows of the perfection Christ would eventually embody. But "These things happened to them as examples and were written down as warnings for us" (I Corinthians 10:11). Unless we see ourselves in the stories—unless we gasp, "Hey, that's just like me!"—we won't heed their warnings or learn from their journeys, lessons, and victories.

Here we need the courage to face our reflection in both the heroes and villains of the Bible. Yes, the villains! Sometimes I'm like David facing a giant or bully. Unfortunately, sometimes I'm the bully, opposing what God is trying to do in the world. Sometimes I'm noble Joseph, trying to protect Mary from a tyrannical King Herod. Other times I'm like tyrannical King Herod, trying to protect my status and position from being threatened.

The Bible may be about God, but he has directed it at you. The scriptures reveal Jesus and reflect on us.

Back to James' Bible study crash course. Look. Look intently. Discern what it says. Over time, as you "continue to do this," you'll start hearing from God.

So don't *just* look. When you've seen something that applies to you and your life, *listen* to the Holy Spirit until you've *heard* him.

As we listen to the Holy Spirit, what God has said becomes what God is saying. What you're reading will become what you're hearing. What happened then becomes what's happening now. He will show you how to *do what it says* in perfect harmony with Jesus, empowered by the Holy Spirit.

What's next? Ask the Holy Spirit for power to obey the word, and then *do it.* That's where the true blessing is found.

Scholarly Bible study can be complicated, but life-changing Bible study is built on this simple progression: *Look, listen, and do.*

Look until you see both Jesus and yourself in what you're reading.

Listen until you hear what to do about it.

Follow through until you've obeyed.

There's more to Bible study than this, but you have access to the same Holy Spirit the authors of the Bible walked with. Jesus promised that when we walk with the Spirit, he will guide us into all truth (John 16:33).

In the next crash course, I'll show you how to get started hearing God's voice personally through his Holy Spirit. As exciting as that may sound, we must learn to honour what God has already spoken and revealed in the scriptures far above these personal revelations. Treasure God's written word, friends. Meditate on it. Marinate your soul in it. Let it challenge, correct, and train you.

You don't love God more than you love his written word.

Period.

15

Hearing God's Voice

Years ago a Christian camp invited me to speak for their teen week. After one of the sessions, two young ladies approached me to ask for guidance and prayer. One of the girls confessed a secret sin that had been smothering her soul with a blanket of shame. Let's call her Sarah.

God had already forgiven Sarah, but she didn't feel forgiven. I remembered Christ's rule: *That we go in peace.* With the shame still raging through her soul, I asked him a simple question: "Lord Jesus, Sarah sinned against you by doing _____, but what would you like her to know about that now?"

Sarah gasped like she'd just lunged back up from the deep end of a dark pool, then sobbed like a baby. When she could put words together, I asked her what was going on.

"He... he spoke to me," she crooned, which prompted another wave of tears. "He spoke to me, he spoke to me." I asked her what he said, and it wasn't anything fancy: "I love you. You're forgiven."

That's it. Five words sent Sarah spinning and healed her heart. That doesn't surprise me, though. In the beginning, "God said, "Let there be light," and there was light" (Genesis 1:3). God's words create worlds!

Learning to discern God's voice is a paradox: On one hand, it's a lifelong journey. On the other hand, a child can get started with beautiful simplicity.

Jesus insists, "My sheep listen to my voice; I know them, and they follow me" (John 10:27). Sheep aren't the brightest creatures, so this is wonderful news. Here's a brief crash course in hearing God to get you started or fine-tune your listening.

First of all, God doesn't just speak. He *communicates.* This is a powerful truth, because it frames hearing God in the broadest possible terms. We cannot not communicate; even silence speaks volumes.

Second, whatever God says is God's word, however he decides to say it. God still speaks, which means I can receive words from God. This does not mean everything we hear God say should be treated as 'scripture-level' revelation. The holy Bible contains the only inerrant, universally true, ultimately authoritative words of God. God will not add to this revelation. He will only elaborate on it or help us understand and apply it.

What I hear God speaking into my life is not inerrant because I'm a flawed vessel. It is not universally true, binding for everyone in all times and places. And it certainly doesn't carry the same authoritative weight as the Bible does. In fact, what I think I'm hearing God say must always be subject to what God has already said in his written word.

God communicates his truth with us in five basic ways. Think of these ways as packages containing the essence of what he's trying to say. If you don't think you hear God, you're probably just focusing on the wrong package.

Package #1: God communicates verbally.

The Bible is the ultimate expression of this package, but the Holy Spirit speaks verbally to our hearts as well. Paul explained the source of his teaching, for example: "We speak, not in words taught us by human wisdom but in words taught by the Spirit, explaining spiritual realities with Spirit-taught words" (I Corinthians 2:13).

God may speak audible words from time to time. I've only heard God's audible voice once in my life. Normally, his Spirit sends his words into our minds. These words may arrive through the books, blog posts, people, songs, movies, or even billboards at the bus stop. The main thing is to notice what God is trying to communicate through his words when they come.

Package #2: God also communicates visually.

God loves to speak through mental images, pictures, or physical things in our environment we can actually see with our eyes. The prophet Habakkuk wrote, "I will look to see what he will say to me" (Habakkuk 2:1). In the same way, watch how Jeremiah's interaction with God unfolded: "The word of the Lord came to me: "What do you see, Jeremiah?" "I see the branch of an almond tree," I replied" (Jeremiah 1:11). In this case, God's word was packaged visually and led to a verbal conversation.

When we pray, images may appear in our minds. This can be God speaking to us. Sometimes I 'see' a friend's face in my mind's eye when God wants me to pray for them or reach out with some kind of encouragement.

Visions and night dreams are also forms of God's visual communication. The entire book of Revelation took this form. Throughout the Bible, believers and enemies of God alike received dreams when the Holy Spirit wanted to communicate something to them.

Package #3: God communicates through our thoughts and logic.

Remember when Peter 'guessed' who Jesus truly was? Jesus replied, "This was not revealed to you by flesh and blood, but by my Father in heaven" (Matthew 16:17).

One of the most common questions I hear about hearing God's voice is, "How do I know if it's God speaking, or just my own thoughts?" That's the wrong question, because God can speak through your thoughts. The Holy Spirit guides us into all truth (John 16:13). This implies an ongoing process of illumination. The Spirit's guidance can happen so subtly that we mistake it for our own thought process. Jesus had to help Peter understand where his flash of insight came from.

As I've already mentioned this throughout this book, my best ideas often 'come to me' when I'm praying. I'm not that smart. This is God speaking to me through logical processes.

Package #4: God communicates through our intuition.

Sometimes we just 'know' things from God. A friend of mine describes this as *knowing in her know-er.* There are no words, pictures, or even logical thoughts attached. We *just know.*

Jesus modelled this beautifully for us. On several occasions in the Gospels, we read that Jesus knew people's thoughts (Matthew 9:4, Luke 9:47). Sometimes God gives us a Holy-Spirit-inpired gut instinct to help us with general guidance. This enables us to discern between good and bad, or sometimes yes or no.

King David sought "yes/no" guidance from the Holy Spirit quite often throughout his life. On one occasion,

> "David inquired of the Lord, "Shall I go and attack the
> Philistines? Will you deliver them into my hands?" The
> Lord answered him, "Go, for I will surely deliver the
> Philistines into your hands.""(I Samuel 5:19)

It's important to note that when God uses this form of divine communication, we don't have to understand what's going on. His leading might not make much sense at the time. Sometimes it just feels right. If what we're sensing doesn't contradict God's word or his nature, we need to honour his communication and guidance by obeying what he puts on our hearts to do or say.

Package #5: God communicates through his actions.

Jesus said his Father's work spoke volumes: "I do not speak on my own authority. Rather, it is the Father, living in me, who is doing his work" (John 14:10). Everything God does carries a message. When God sent Jesus, that said something! When God heals, provides, or blesses us, each blessing carries a message from heaven.

The other day my wife left me a package of praline pecans on the counter. I smiled when I saw it. Simple gestures like this transcend the actual gift. The treat carried a heart-felt message: "I was thinking of you. You matter to me. I love you." In the same way, when God gives us something, the provision carries a message from his heart to yours.

An answered prayer is a reply from God. He's answering one or more of your questions by responding to your request. An answered prayer for provision carries a loving "Yes!" from God. If God doesn't answer a prayer the way we'd like, that's a "No," a "Not yet," or a "Not like that."

God's actions speak clearly enough that he holds us accountable for getting his message. As the writer to the Hebrews remarked,

> "Today, if you hear his voice, do not harden your hearts
> as you did in the rebellion, during the time of testing in
> the wilderness, where your ancestors tested and tried
> me, though for forty years they saw what I did"
> (Hebrews 3:7-9).

The Hebrews heard God's voice for forty years through what he did. Throughout scripture, he communicated through open doors, closed doors, miracles, and even disasters.

We should be careful what we 'read into' God's actions. It's important not to jump to conclusions about what our circumstances are saying. In one situation, facing opposition might be a sign to slow down or change course. In another circumstance, God might be telling us to bear down to persevere through a battle.

Solomon's golden principle bears repeating here: "Trust in the Lord with all your heart and lean not on your own understanding; in all your ways submit to him, and he will make your paths straight" (Proverbs 3:5,6). As I get older, I'm gradually learning that my natural leaning or 'discernment' is often wrong. I usually need more straightening out than my path does!

Putting the packages together

When God communicates, he uses one or more of these five packages. The more we're aware of the options open to him, the more likely we are to identify messages from him.

The Holy Spirit also likes to send these packages through a variety of carriers. I can't count how many times people have either intentionally or unknowingly passed along something God wanted me to hear. Biblically, God has used angels for this purposes. Once he even gave a donkey the ability to speak to get the attention of a particularly stubborn prophet.

Quite often, he deploys the five packages in combination.

As I read his word (verbal) I imagine what the scripture is illuminating (visual). Things just start making sense to me (logical). Along the way, I sense his conviction (intuition) and respond by putting the word into practice. God then blesses my obedience (actions), at which point I sense his joy (intuition). The fruit of this? His word makes even more sense to me (logical). See what I mean?

Another key insight: We all hear God differently. You may receive more visual communication, while your friend discerns God's voice more intuitively. People who hear God through their logic tend to think God doesn't speak to them because they're waiting for a train of words to traipse through their minds. I also think we can learn to hear God with a broader spectrum as we become aware of the other packages.

Ask the Holy Spirit to awaken you to the full spectrum of his voice. Then listen—and look—for what God wants to say to you.

The Temple Pathway will teach you to become more intentional about hearing God. I would encourage you to invite God to communicate with you, then put your pen to the page, trusting he will speak. Record what comes to mind. Write down what you're hearing.

What if we get it wrong? Don't stress; it happens often! The beauty of writing things down is that we can circle back on it later to test the word we think God sent, holding it up to biblical filters.

As Jesus said, "Man shall not live by bread alone, but by every word that comes from the mouth of God" (Matthew 4:4). Hearing his voice is your daily bread. There is no option but to learn to hear him well, and the Temple Pathway is the perfect place to learn. It teaches us to do what the prophet Habakkuk modelled for us:

> "I will stand at my watch and station myself on the ramparts; I will look to see what he will say to me, and what answer I am to give to this complaint. Then the Lord replied: "Write down the revelation and make it plain on tablets so that a herald may run with it." (Habakkuk 2:1,2)

I credit Mark Virkler with introducing me to Habakkuk's basic process. Biblical saints and prophets throughout the ages have followed a similar track. Let's unpack it briefly here.

1. **"I will stand at my watch and station myself on the ramparts."**
Apparently Habakkuk's 'prayer closet' was located on the city walls.

He set up a time, space, and place for God. But he didn't just 'show up,' he *stationed* himself. He prepared to receive from God by putting a blank tablet on his lap and quill in his hand. In the same way, we give God our full attention, with blank journal pages waiting for his word to us.

2. **"What answer I am to give to this complaint."** Habakkuk may have come with a blank tablet, but he didn't come with a blank mind. Chapter one is full of questions levelled at God—complaints —and now he's waiting to see what God has to say about them. In other words, he began with *Ascent*—venting his heart to God.

It's important to take the time to tease out the questions lurking beneath our angst and present them to God. If we don't, those questions will drive us to seek answers in unhelpful and unholy places. When God shares his truth with us, we use that truth to meet our struggles. Jesus modelled this when he was tempted by the devil (Matthew 4:1-11).

3. **"I will look to see what he will say to me."** Looking activates seeing because we tend to see more of what we're looking for. Habakkuk anticipated a response. In the same way, we fix our eyes on Jesus, and wait expectantly for his answer to our questions. I recommend two starting blocks: Picturing Jesus on his throne, or asking the Holy Spirit to show you where Jesus is in your problem. Look to him to see what he will say to you.

4. **"Write down the revelation and make it plain on tablets so that a herald may run with it."** Moses. David. Solomon. The prophets. Matthew, Mark, Luke, John, and Paul—they'd all discovered the power of writing down what God says to us.

When God impresses a Bible verse on my heart, I don't just read it, I write it down. The simple act of putting pen to paper activates my faith in profound ways. I expect God to speak, especially when I ask him a question. Please, please try this, even if you don't like writing.

When you write it down, you don't have to memorize it. You can review it. Writing down God's word makes it portable, so you can "do what it says" and run with it (James 1:22).

Some Christians assert that God only speaks through the Bible. The Bible never says that. God never says anything remotely like, "This is God, signing off. It's been a slice. Read my book." Holding this view requires elaborate theological backflips in order to bend scripture into saying what it doesn't say.

Other believers hold a passive-aggressive posture toward God's voice. They may concede that he speaks apart from (and in perfect harmony with) the scriptures, but are scared to go there because they might get deceived. The devil is a prowling lion, seeking whom he might devour, so they'd rather stick to the Bible, thank you very much.

The irony here is painful. Our ongoing battle with a cunning deceiver is precisely what makes hearing God personally so vital! Jesus declared, "Man shall not live by bread alone, but by every word that comes *(ongoing, present tense!)* from the mouth of God." He speaks these words while being tempted by the devil (Matthew 4:1-11). We need to know and hear God's voice *because* there are spiritual strangers, thieves and wolves lurking about (John 10:1-18). We are surrounded by spiritual enemies seeking to steal, kill, and destroy us. The only path through that minefield is to follow the voice of our Shepherd.

You might protest, "Well, I've done just fine without that so far." Dear one, if you've ruled out God speaking to you personally, you've already been deceived. The devil isn't merely hellbent on leading us into heinous sin; he's just as focused on leading us away from intimacy with our beautiful saviour. We must guard ourselves from becoming like the tragic Narnian dwarves in The Last Battle, written by C.S. Lewis. Aslan remarked that,

"They will not let us help them. They have chosen cunning instead of belief. Their prison is only in their own minds, yet they are in that prison; and so afraid of being taken in that they cannot be taken out."

The best way to start growing in your sensitivity to God's voice is to put the faith, hope and love you already have into action. As you're faithful with what God has already said, he will share more of his heart with you. We need to learn to live by every word that comes from his mouth, starting right now.

Remember, God's goal in our intimate interactions with him is to become more fully his so we live, move, and speak like his Son Jesus. I love how Preston Morrison, pastor of Pillar Church, puts it: "God always agrees with himself, and often disagrees with me." If what you think is God's voice never challenges your thinking, you're not listening to the true God.

16

How to Start A Prayer Journal

In this chapter, I'm going to try to convince you to start prayer journalling. Or to give it one more try.

I kid you not, prayer-journalling can double or even triple the long-term spiritual impact of the Temple Pathway. It's that powerful. If you already keep a prayer journal, the method I'm going to teach you will take your journalling to the next level. Not everyone enjoys writing, but I truly believe:

1. Second only to the Holy Spirit, the most influential writer in your life is you.

2. Second only to the Bible, the most important book in your life is your prayer journal.

A prayer journal is a written record of your friendship with God. Scripturally speaking, the Psalms and prophetic books are pretty much collections of Holy-Spirit-inspired prayer journal entries. In fact, nineteen of the Bible's sixty-six book anthology record a form of prayer journalling. They display intimate, life-changing interactions between a loving God and people just like you and me.

Aside from Bible reading and prayer, prayer journalling is the single most important thing I do for my own spiritual growth. I've kept a daily prayer journal for more than thirty years. Those journals record my rich history with God and are some of my most prized possessions.

If you studied your way through the book of Revelation, you would find calls to action like these placed throughout: "*Write* on a scroll what you see... *Write*, therefore, what you have seen... *Write* this... *Write* this down, for these words are trustworthy and true..."

Writing down what God teaches us is life-changing. Over three decades, I have developed and honed a powerful method for prayer journalling I'm confident will lift your relationship with Jesus to new heights. If you still need some convincing, here are five tangible benefits you can expect to gain from this vital practice.

Prayer journalling helps you track your progress in life. When you write significant things down, you can flip back in time to reflect on how you've grown (or not). I love re-reading old journals to see what I struggled with in the past and how different that struggle feels now, in the present. I've found that without a sense of movement or progress in our faith, we lose heart—or lose interest.

Prayer journalling captures the lessons you've learned and truths God has taught you. I have a mini-library of sixty-four journals on my shelf, full of what God has taught me through the years. I don't have to remember it all because I can review what I've learned and rekindle the fires God lit in me.

Prayer journalling records answers to prayer, along with moments of victory and praise. My journals are treasure troves of encouragement when I need to give my faith a reminder of God's faithfulness. My history with God is tangible. I have a living proof of our friendship that I can draw upon when life gets especially hard.

Prayer journalling helps you clarify what's bouncing around in your soul. It provides a way to nail down what I'm feeling, what I'm thinking, why things bother me, and what God's marching orders are. Finding words for what's unclear or painful gives us a certain power over them. Prayer journalling helps clear the haze of confusion and questions.

Prayer journalling is cathartic. Getting things off your chest and into God's hands through written prayer is worth its weight in gold. Writing things down moves our struggles from *invisible* and *internal* to *visible* and *external*. This can help give us objectivity and perspective we can't get by circling endlessly our own minds.

My prayer journalling process

Simply put, I record my interactions with God through all five phases of the Temple Pathway. I use a few key symbols in the margins to highlight what kind of entry I'm recording. This helps me stay focused and to find things I've written when I'm scanning for specific items I want to circle back on. Here is my symbol map:

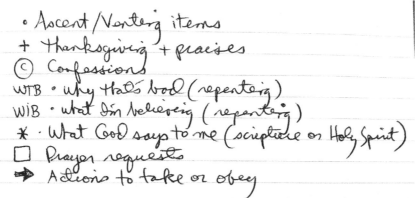

First, I address God personally and record the date. Dating your entry is important for tracking what you learn, noting when prayer requests were answered, and more. You can be creative as you address him: Father, my King, etc:

1. Ascent. Just list whatever comes to mind (and how you're feeling about it).

There's no need to be poetic. I use bullet points, and I don't always use complete sentences. We'll come back to these items later on, when our head and heart are in a better place.

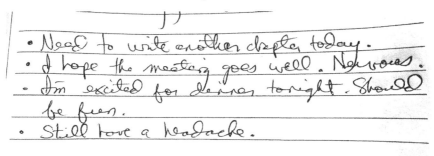

2 & 3. Thanksgiving and Praises. Remember to try and include one thanksgiving related to what God has done through Jesus (the gospel), plus one "thanks ahead of time" entry to grow your faith:

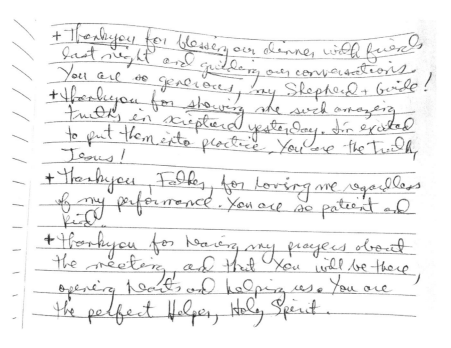

Next up: The Court of Priests, where we'll move through three important steps: Heart-check, confession, and giving/receiving grace.

4. Heart Check. I begin by asking the Holy Spirit to guide me into all truth (John 16:13). I imagine coming into God's searching light (I John 1:9). Then I let him walk me through my recent words, actions, and attitudes.

Along the way, I ask him two important questions. God will highlight what he wants to deal with that day, so I follow his leading:

1. **How have I grieved your heart (through something I've done)?**
2. **How have I quenched your work (through things I failed to do)?**

5. Confession. When God shows me a sin, I confess it, agreeing with his conviction by naming it on paper—without excuse or explanation:

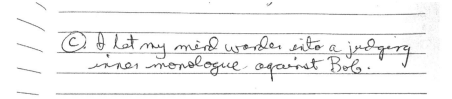

If the sin I'm confessing is a regular occurrence (in this case, a judgmental inner monologue) it means that owning my behaviour is not enough to change it. I need to repent. Please see my crash course on Repentance in the next chapter for an in-depth dive into this vital process.

6. Giving and Receiving Grace

Giving and receiving grace involves three important actions: Forgiving people who hurt us, receiving God's forgiveness for our own sins, and listening to God for his affirmation.

Forgiving others

First, I may need to admit that Bob hurt me. Perhaps my judgmental attitude is a defensive response to him undermining me at work. So I pour out my soul to God, venting my emotions as I go:

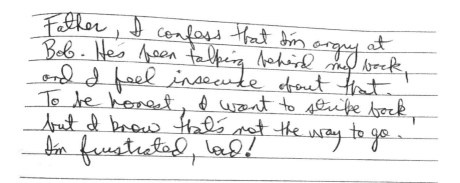

Father, I confess that I'm angry at Bob. He's been talking behind my back, and I feel insecure about that. To be honest, I want to strike back but I know that's not the way to go. I'm frustrated, Lord!

Next, I speak out my forgiveness, give Jesus permission to lift away my my anger and frustration towards Bob, and ask him to do it. With the eyes of my heart, I see it being done and thank him.

Afterwards, I take a moment to revisit the conflict and see how my view of Bob (including my feeling toward him) have changed. Often my negative emotions are gone. Other times, I circle back around and go deeper with how I'm feeling, until my heart towards Bob is full of God's grace for him.

Forgiving myself

Next, I give Jesus permission to come lift away my own guilt and shame about the sin I've confessed. I work through the same process, naming how I feel about myself—anger, disappointment, guilt, shame—and ask him to come lift them away. With the eyes of my heart, I see this being done and thank him. I take a moment to relish his grace and forgiveness.

Receiving God's affirmation

Next, I simply quiet my heart and ask, "Father, is there anything I said or did that pleased You yesterday? Would you please reveal that to me?"

He nearly always brings something to my attention. Sometimes I recall a moment or a decision I made from the previous day. When he brings something up, I ask him about it: "What pleased you about that?" I write down what he says and thank him for his encouragement:

> * "Bradley, I love how you let go of your plans and desires for the day and just let yourself flow with Shaira's needs instead. You looked to me for guidance, for strength, for grace, and I blessed you for it."
>
> thankyou, Jesus. You are so good and kind.

7. **Revelation.** Next up, I imagine myself walking into the Holy Place, where I will receive God's revelation and respond with Spirit-led prayer. The showbread / bread of the presence is the place where I review (and speak out) God's word and promises. If I've written them down in previous journal entries, I re-read them, speaking them in prayer to God. Or I just declare what I know to be true:

> "Father, thankyou in advance for what You will do. You have provided, You are providing, and You will provide, because You are MY PROVIDER. Amen!

I also inject biblical faith logic into any issues that still intimidate me. Faith logic, you'll recall, is projecting God's past faithfulness and power into our current needs:

> You provided for us when we were living between homes. You provided strength when we were weak. You are providing right now, even if I can't see it. You never fail us!

This is also the point where I study God's word. My heart is now in the right place to receive the learning, correction, and faith-building I need. My study becomes an extension of our ongoing conversation. God's words to me are in quotes, so I can distinguish them from my own thoughts:

> * I Peter 5:8: "Be alert and of sober mind. Your enemy the devil prowls around like a roaring lion looking for someone to devour."
>
> Interesting — In 4:7 Peter says "be alert and of sober mind so that you may pray."
>
> He knows what he's talking about, doesn't He, Jesus? He fell asleep on you in the garden, and then fell into temptation. He got devoured.

Bible study isn't an exercise, it's a conversation. Record what God says to you as you study, and ask him about it. Write down what you believe he's saying to you in reply. It could come as words, a thought, a mental picture, another scripture, or even a feeling. When you've written it down, you can test it (does it jive with the rest of scripture?) and follow up with more questions, as needed. Often God will reveal something to me and I'll ask for clarification.

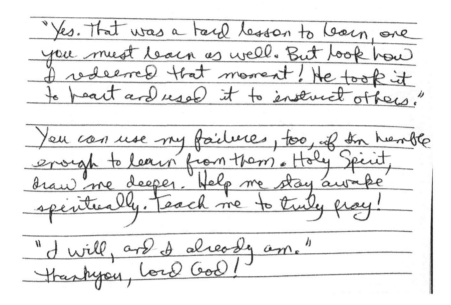

He also helps me apply the word to my life by choosing an action to accompany my learning:

When your prayer journal becomes a live record of your actual relationship with God, you'll be hooked for good. But there's more!

God will illuminate his truth throughout the Temple Pathway, but his light seems to shine brighter, the further up and further in we go.

It never ceases to amaze me how much insight and wisdom 'occurs to me' in the Holy Place. This isn't me figuring things out. God is speaking to me and renewing my mind to resonate with his. And why shouldn't insights increase by the time I reach the Holy Place? I'm a different person than the one who started this process in the *Ascent* phase.

This is where I circle back around to the issues I vented in my *Ascent*, inviting the Holy Spirit to speak into them. To review, my *Ascent* at the beginning of my Temple Pathway looked like this:

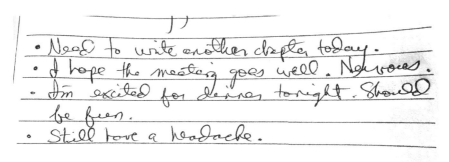

Now I briefly revisit each of these items, pausing to see if God has any hindsight, insight, or foresight to give me. At this point it's fairly common to realize a few things on my list no longer even matter to me anymore. I pray a simple prayer here: "Is there anything You want me to know about this? How about this?" Then I write down what comes to mind:

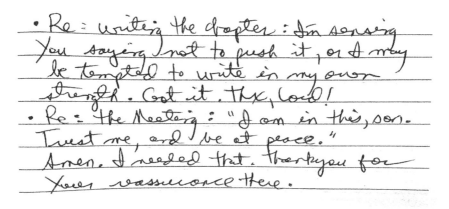

God may also speak into other areas of my life, and I write this down, too. His words are daily bread. Writing them down in my journal honours God and helps me keep his word.

9. Spirit-led prayer. Spirit-led prayer is prayer grounded in the gospel, informed by faith in God's character, promises, and his word. It is prayer infused with Holy-Spirit insight, revelation, and confidence.

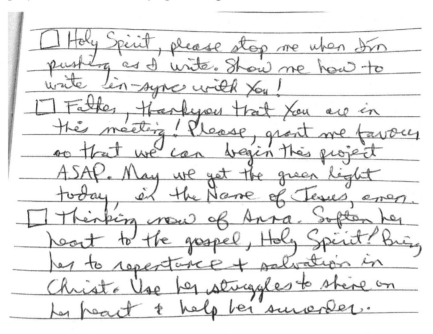

Sometimes I write my prayers down, sometimes not. When I do record my prayers, I try to jot down the heart of them, with checkboxes beside them. Why? Because when I go back and review, I can check the boxes with answers to prayer, and add a brief note about how God answered. I take these back into thanksgiving and praise. The upward spiral continues!

Sometimes God inspires us to pray faster or longer than we could keep up with on paper. In that case, let go of writing things down. I might come back and summarize later, if I think it's important.

10. Worship. Finally, for the finale, we step into the Holy of Holies to worship God for who he is.

I don't always write this part down, unless God reveals something significant. Many days, I just enjoy a 'hug from heaven,' sing to God, or rest in his love. Sometimes I slide off my couch and worship him face-down, on the ground, revelling in his beauty and glory. If he reveals something important, I jot it down and pray through it. At some point, my heart is at rest. I'm focused on Jesus and ready for my day.

I hope this chapter helped you see how powerful journalling your way through the Temple Pathway can be. You'll probably want to tweak it for your own walk with God. My encouragement is just to start, keep it up for a month straight, and see what happens. Here are three more 'power-tips' for you to consider in your prayer journalling:

One: Create a table of contents at the beginning of your journal. I typically reserve one or two lined pages (2-4 sides) at the beginning of my journal for this purpose. I record a brief description of what I've learned, plus the date it appears in my journal. This creates a simple way to find "that thing I learned about prayer and fasting" without having to scour the entire journal for it.

I also put an asterisk (*) beside the entries referring to dreams, or ones that seem to be especially prophetic about my life and future. Here is a peek at the actual index of one of my journals:

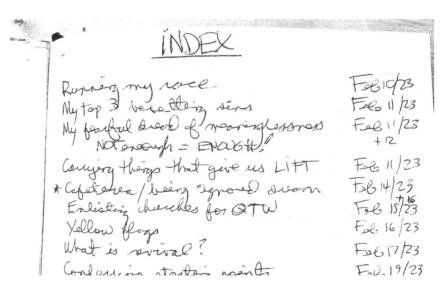

Two: Make it a habit to review the prior week. This will help you remember God's word, track patterns in your struggles, and help you evaluate whether you followed through on what you learned. Pay attention to your arrows, those 'action items' you committed to!

Three: Take time at the end of December to read your entire year's worth of journal entries. I've been doing this for as long as I can remember and it's game-changing. You'll find themes you forgot about. You'll dust off promises you still need today, commitments you forgot to keep, victories you need to remember. What I do while I review is create a list of the top lessons of the previous year. I then 'bring' these with me into the new year as a way of building on what's gone before.

If you'd like to download a free PDF that outlines this exact process and adds a few more helpful steps and ideas, click here or scan this QR code. You don't need to keep a prayer journal to benefit from this tool.

Would you like some help learning to prayer journal through the Temple Pathway? Pick up the Temple Pathway Journal on Amazon, a 30-day guided experience that will equip you to launch a prayer journal of your own!

17

Repentance

Have you ever found yourself confessing the same sins to God repeatedly, or apologizing to people for the same sins over and over? Do you ever wonder why you keep getting sucked into the same negative patterns and mistakes?

I have good news: you're about to find out why lasting life-change never seems to stick. You're going to learn how to break the sin-cycle by accessing the power of the gospel in your life.

So far in the Court of Priests, we've unpacked the power of confession and forgiveness: "If we confess our sins, he is faithful and just and will forgive our sins" (I John 1:9). This exchange is pictured by the bloody altar in the diagram pictured above. But God also wants to "purify us from all unrighteousness."

That internal cleansing is what the giant basin is all about.

Confession is like admitting we've got rotten fruit growing on our tree. But confession doesn't fix the rot. Confession plucks bad fruit from the branches year after year, wondering why the tree keeps producing a bad crop. What we need is genuine repentance. Repentance takes an ax to the roots of the tree; it gets to the source of the corruption and cuts it out (Luke 3:8,9).

Repentance is a change of mind that changes our ways. The *ability* to repent begins as a gift from God (II Timothy 2:25), and that ability gives us the power to respond. Our response to that ability—our *response-ability*—is to meet God in his transforming work. This is why Jesus also framed repentance as a command: "Repent and believe the good news" (Mark 1:15).

Repentance is not just feeling sorry for what we did. It's much more than saying, "I repent" while meaning well. True repentance is a process of self-discovery that helps us understand what needs to change in us:

1. Why what we did was bad
2. Why we did what we did: The false beliefs that feed the sinful behaviour
3. What we need to do to break free from our sin cycle
4. The gospel truths that set us free from the false beliefs
5. What we need to do to clean up our mess

Notice that I said repentance is a *process*. That's because genuine transformation unfolds as an ongoing conversation with God. He reveals something I need to see. I respond with surrender. He reveals something deeper. I say "yes" to him again. Eventually we get to the root, the source of the problem. Repentance changes my *ways* by changing my *why*—the thoughts and intentions of my heart.

The deeper I let him go, the more profound and lasting the changes will be. The more destructive the sin, the deeper (and longer) the repentance process will need to go. Telling lies when you feel cornered is damaging, but not as destructive as sexual predation. You get the idea.

I've been recovering from burnout the past year and a half. No one "did it to me." I did it to myself. That's my *confession*. What I found interesting, though, was a comment I heard multiple times from my burnout coach and counsellor: "You're very self-aware."

On one hand, I had to laugh; my burnout was proof that I was at least partly blind to my harmful ways of living and the false beliefs that motivated them. On the other hand, processing my soul with Jesus (and working through the repentance process for countless struggles over the years) has given me a certain clarity about my weaknesses. It's also given me insight into what to do with those self-revelations.

Throughout my journey, the Holy Spirit helped me develop a set of key questions that guide me through the repentance process. My method is not the only way to repent, but God has used it as a powerful tool to process my flaws and failures with him. It helps me get to the heart of my faulty thinking so he can replace it with his liberating truth. My soul is changing over time. With my soul on the mend, my life follows suit. I trust this will become your experience as well.

Resisting arrest

Some folks avoid facing their faults and failures at all costs. Many people hide their flaws and struggles from others, presenting an "I'm fine" persona to the world. Some people even self-justify their destructive behaviours: "That's just how or who I am!" To others, owning their failures and flaws feels like death.

At its root, 'resisting arrest' is a fear of shame. Guilt owns the fact that *I did something bad.* Shame is different; it believes *I am bad—and if people saw it, if they only knew, they'd reject me and I'd be all alone.* Ever since Adam and Eve felt ashamed of their nakedness and hid behind a pathetic 'fruit of the loom' fig leaf, we've all been tempted to do the same. Jesus said,

> "Light has come into the world, but people loved darkness instead of light because their deeds were evil. Everyone who does evil hates the light, and will not come into the light for fear that their deeds will be exposed. But whoever lives by the truth comes into the light, so that it may be seen plainly that what they have done has been done in the sight of God" (John 3:19-21).

Sometimes we press ourselves into God's light just enough to confess our sin, but stop there. We taste the relief of God's grace and forgiveness, but quickly retreat into the shadows before things get more intense and uncomfortable. God wants to go deeper—*much* deeper. King David wrote, "Behold, you delight in truth in the inward being, and you teach me wisdom in the secret heart" (Psalm 51:6, ESV). This is where freedom is found:

> "For the word of God is alive and active. Sharper than any double-edged sword, it penetrates even to dividing soul and spirit, joints and marrow; it judges the thoughts and attitudes of the heart" (Hebrews 4:12).

Multiple sessions with my Counsellor and Burnout Coach led me into some helpful insights and challenging mirror moments. Some of these revelations hurt because exposed flaws in my thinking and uncovered hidden insecurities. They took me to places where I was trusting in something or someone other than God. At the root, the Holy Spirit showed me many of the *whys* behind my *whats*.

It wasn't flattering, let me tell you.

I welcomed every one of these revelations. Why? God rewards surrender to his deep surgery with big, bold, beautiful freedom. As a result, the truths that cut became a vital part of my healing and repentance process. Because I welcomed God's deep work on my operating system, I'm confident I won't descend this path into burnout again.

The repentance process is so powerful and important that I dedicated this entire chapter to unpacking it. Let's get started.

The repentance process

Before we get into the how, let's review: True repentance is a process of self-discovery that helps us understand five things:

1. Why what we did was bad
2. Why we did what we did: The false beliefs that fed the sinful behaviour
3. What we need to do to break free from our sin cycle
4. The gospel truths that set us free from the false beliefs
5. What we need to do to clean up our mess

Repentance walks us through each of these five steps in turn. I highly recommend writing all of this down so you can keep track. To be honest, prayer journalling is the best way to make the most of this journey. It adds a powerful sixth step: Circling back later to follow-through and see how you're doing with implementing the solution.

I don't think you should try to work through these steps with every sin you commit. Try to focus on your *ways*. Those transgressions will always come from a deeper root God wants to address. As you spend time in the Temple Pathway, your ways will become obvious to you because sins will repeat themselves. At that point, you can dive into repentance as needed.

Repentance begins with a sin or way we've already confessed (either something we did or didn't do). The idea is to turn each of the five steps into a question. You can direct the question to both yourself and God:

1. Why is that bad? (I abbreviate with **WTB** on paper).
2. What lie am I believing? (**WIB?**)
3. What is the truth I need to hear?
4. What do I need to do in order to be free from this power?
5. What do I need to do to make this right?

Why is that bad? (WTB?)

When we ask these questions, the answer may seem too obvious to mention at first: "Why is that bad? Because I shouldn't have lost my temper, that's why!" But that's a surface answer. What we'll do is ask these questions several times, peeling back the layers, hopefully going deeper each time. Ask the Holy Spirit to guide you into all truth as you repent.

The "Why is that bad?" question is designed to expose two major culprits: The sin beneath the sin, and the damage we caused. Both tracks should be subjected to the five questions.

Author and therapist Danny Silk uses an analogy for "the damage we caused" that I find extremely helpful. He says when we sin, the impact is a lot like dropping a can of fresh paint on the floor. We can imagine the pigment splattering all around us. Everyone and everything that has paint on them has been affected by our mistake and must be included when we take responsibility for our sin.

The sin beneath the sin will generally be some version of, "I was trying to _____." To show you what I mean, let's start walking through the repentance process, focusing on uncovering that dangerous root.

CONFESSION: I totally lost it on my kids today.

Next, we ask ourselves (and the Holy Spirit), *Why is that bad?* (WTB). Trust me, you probably don't fully see it yet. Write down the answer that comes to you:

WTB: I gave in to anger again.

Next we ask the "Why is *that* bad?" question of our *last answer*, but go a little deeper: *Why was it bad that you gave in to anger again? What were you trying to do?* Record what comes to your mind:

WTB: I was trying to make them obey me by intimidating them.

Ouch. You may have to ask this question several times to get to a root like this, but let's say we've got it. Now that we see what we were trying to do and see how wrong that was, we ask other question: *What must I believe (WIB) at some level, for me to try to make my kids obey me through intimidation?*

Please note: We're not looking for what's logically true or false at this point. We're trying to uncover what *feels* true (even if it's false). And we're not trying to justify anything, because our behaviour is always driven by our emotionally rooted beliefs. So again: *What must I believe at some level, for me to try to make my kids obey me through intimidation?*

WIB: That I *needed* to control them.

That's good. But we ask the question again, trying to go deeper: *Why did I believe I needed to control them?* Here you may come up with a few options:

WIB: Because being out of control scares me.

WIB: Because I need to be in control.

That seems important. So, *What must I **also** believe, if I believe I need to be in control?*

WIB: That God isn't in control, or that I can't trust him to handle this.

Boom. That's the heart of it, the sin beneath the sin—us trying to be god of our own lives in some way. The sin beneath the sin is anything or anyone that dethrones Christ in our thinking or actions.

When you uncover the root lie, your heart may recoil in disgust over what you find. That's part of the repentance process. We're not just sorry for what we did, but find ourselves repelled by the lie we were believing. Don't worry, this disgust is temporary. Be sure to direct your loathing toward your sin, not yourself.

This is when you need to vocalize your rejection of the sin and the lie. Both the lies we believe and sin we indulge hold power over us. First we own them through confession, then we disown them through renunciation. As children of God, we have authority to tear down those lies and break with the spiritual power the sin held over us (II Corinthians 10:3-5).

Proverbs 28:13 says, "Whoever conceals their sins does not prosper, but the one who confesses and renounces them finds mercy." Sinful ways and patterns must be renounced for us to live in true freedom. Sin is not just disobedience. It is a spiritual power that seeks to "have" us (Genesis 4:7). Paul writes that "you are slaves of the one you obey—whether you are slaves to sin, which leads to death, or to obedience, which leads to righteousness" (Romans 6:16).

Renouncing sin is about breaking our willing partnership with its power. It vocalizes our allegiance to Jesus and declares that we don't want any of sin's effects and influences to persist in our mind, will, and emotions.

Paul admonishes us to "put to death" the misdeeds of the flesh by the power of the Holy Spirit (Romans 8:13). In fact, he says, we must "Put to death, therefore, *whatever* belongs to your earthly nature" (Colossians 3:5). Our old nature is crucified with Christ, but our souls are full of thoughts, values, and habits 'belonging' to that nature. As we repent, we cast these off like old clothing and "clothe" ourselves with the virtues of Jesus (Colossians 3:12).

If I were working through the repentance process for losing it on my kids, I'd pray a prayer something like this, out loud:

> "In the name of Jesus, Father, I reject the lie that I have to be in control, or that You aren't trustworthy or powerful. I reject and break the power of control in every area of my life and cast it away from me. I claim total freedom from every manifestation of that evil power in my body, soul, and spirit. In Jesus' name, amen."

I often visualize this happening as I pray it, using the imagery of ripping off a disgusting, old sweater and tossing it at the feet of Jesus (similar to the imagery Paul uses in Colossians 3:9,10).

The next step in the process is inviting God to speak the truth you need to hear into the emotionally charged lie you've just uncovered. It's important to acknowledge that *part of you believes that lie*, even if most of you doesn't. It's the part that believes the lie we're addressing here:

> "Lord Jesus, I open myself and every part of me to your truth right now. Would you come and speak to this wounded part of me that believes it needs to be in

control and can't trust you? What is the truth I need to hear about this?"

God may bring up scriptures that display this truth. He may speak words into your mind: "I've got this. I've got you. You don't need to be in control." He may give you a powerful picture or analogy, ground you again in scripture, or send peace directly into your heart.

Whatever God reveals is the truth, so thank and praise him—then declare it out loud. Paul says, "Since we have the same spirit of faith according to what has been written, "I believed, and so I spoke," we also believe, and so we also speak" (I Corinthians 4:13). So that's what we do, too.

This is all pretty amazing, but we're not done yet. We still have some paint to clean up, remember? Let's quickly go through the same process again, with "the damage we caused" in view:

C: I lost it on my kids again today

WTB (damage): I could see they were afraid of me and my anger

WTB: I hurt their feelings and belittled them, and they feel insecure around me now

WTB: I have damaged their trust and our relationship

WIB: That me being right is more important than our relationship, or their hearts

TRUTH GOD REVEALS: My kids and our relationship are more important than any issue

Once we've seen the truth about the damage we caused, we ask God the final question in the repentance process: *What do I need to do to clean up this mess or make things right?*

This might involve confessing my sin to my kids and asking for their forgiveness. If our sin has been particularly destructive, we may need to pay for physical damages, begin radical accountability, seek out professional help, remove ourselves from a tempting situation, or even report ourselves to the police. If you aren't willing to make things right, you're not done repenting.

But let's return to the analogy with our kiddos. When we confess our sin to them, we put the repentance-damage process into our own words (age appropriately, of course):

> "Hey guys. I totally lost it on you with my anger today. I could see that made you afraid of me. I hurt your feelings and made you feel bad. You probably feel unsafe around me now, and I don't blame you. I know I damaged your trust and our relationship. You probably feel like being right is more important to me than our relationship is, but that's not true. You, and our relationship, are more important than any issue. I'm so sorry. Would you please forgive me?"

Next, we let those we've hurt help set appropriate boundaries and next steps. Danny Silk's incredible book, *Unpunishable*, gave me this idea. It's not right to make our kids hug us if they're not ready, for example. In terms of next steps, we may ask, *What happens next? Are you okay? Are we okay? Is there anything you want me to do to make this right?*

There are obviously exceptions to this approach, but if we're not willing to submit to the wounded party's suggestions, we're still making the issue about us. Our humility and submission prove our repentance. It's also important to follow through on what they recommend, if at all possible.

When you're dealing with adults or older kids, sharing the 'sin beneath the sin' confession may help rebuild some trust in your relationship. When you do this, don't include any critiques of the other party. And please don't slip in a line about how they "made you" do what you did. You are accountable for you, full stop. Leave their part to them and to God, or bring it up at another time if necessary.

Your confession might look like this:

> "I want you to know that I see things more clearly now. When I lost it on you with my anger, I was trying to control you. Feeling out-of-control scares me, so part of me believes I need to be in control all the time. That's not trusting God to take care of me. I see now that because Jesus is in control, I don't have to be. That's a relief! I've rejected those lies and invited the Holy Spirit to seal these truths into my heart. Please pray for me as I grow through this and hold me accountable when you see it happening again. I want to leave that old habit behind forever."

You may find that after your confessions, the other party lets their guard down to apologize for their part. If they don't, it's okay—that's not what you're responsible for.

I think you can see how powerful and deep this process is. That said, think of what I've shared as a tool to guide your cooperation with the Spirit, not a formula you can run with to "get it done."

Check out the Toolbox page on my Deeply Devoted website for a repentance process summary and a downloadable PDF you can store on your mobile devices for easy access.

Here is a quick summary of the entire process, simplified:

1. Own why what you did was bad by asking **WTB** (Why is that bad?) until you find the sin beneath the sin (the root).

2. Ask **WIB** until you find the lie driving that sin beneath the sin.

3. Renounce and reject the power of that sin, including all its influences and effects on your mind, will, and emotions. Reaffirm your allegiance to Jesus.

4. Ask the Holy Spirit to reveal what he wants you to know about the sin beneath the sin and the lies that drove that behaviour.

5. Go through the above process again, this time aimed at exploring the damage you caused, so you can ask for forgiveness and take steps to clean up the mess you made.

Join me in this mission!

Deeply Devoted isn't just a book, it's a ministry with a mission: to help believers in Jesus grow a lifestyle of intimacy with God. I truly believe this material has the potential to transform thousands of hearts, churches, and organizations. And that's my prayer. I'd love to see a quiet time revolution sweep the Church!

If you believe in this mission too, here are some next steps. Just tap or scan the QRs to learn more.

1. **Did this book challenge, inspire, or change you?** Take a few minutes to write a review on Amazon.

2. <u>Subscribe to my newsletter.</u> I send out a weekly email with tips from the trenches of my own relationship with God. If you want to keep growing deeper with Jesus, sign up today!

3. <u>Become a prayer and/or financial partner.</u> You can be a part of growing this ministry! Prayer partners receive a weekly email with strategic prayer requests. Three-quarters of my salary and expenses come through generous financial partnership from people just like you.

4. <u>Your church, camp, or organization can benefit, too!</u> Are you a pastor or leader? I would love to help your church/organization get intentional about intimacy with God. *Deeply Devoted* offers workshops, Small Group studies,

and more. Interested? Let's chat about how *Deeply Devoted* can help your church go deeper with Jesus.

Also by Brad Huebert

The Temple Pathway Journal is a 30 day guided experience that trains you to journal your way through the Temple Pathway in your daily time with Jesus. By the end of the month, you'll be ready to launch a powerful prayer journal of your own.

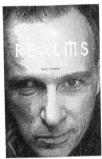

Realms - Imagine waking up in the spiritual realm, where everything you've taken by faith is now visible to your eyes. This allegory will help you exchange your striving for a life of grace in God's kingdom. Experience an infusion of fresh faith, hope, and love that will change your life.

Beloved - Beloved re-tells the story of the Bible as a true fairy tale. Experience the wonder of seeing the biblical story through fresh eyes. Your love for Jesus and trust in him as Lord and Saviour will soar to new heights through this simple story.

Prophetic - Learn the biblical foundations for prophecy and the prophetic in the life of everyday people just like you and me. And do it without getting weird! In this short book you'll learn how God speaks, what the prophetic is for, how to speak the words God gives you, and how to receive words from God when they come from someone else.

Made in United States
Orlando, FL
01 December 2024

54765803R00125